1

Introducing the Gospel of Globalism

Understanding the secular narrative for 2020 and beyond.

By Jess Gjerstad

Introducing the Gospel of Globalism: Understanding the Secular narrative for 2020 and beyond.

Printed by: CreateSpace an Amazon.com company
Charleston SC

https://kdp.amazon.com/en_US/

Cover by: Joshua Fenimore
Instagram.com/Joshua_Fenimore

5

6

TABLE OF CONTENTS

8

Chapter 1- The Covington Incident- an example of the nationalist problem?

The mainstream media had waited years for this moment: Finally, an example of everything wrong with American white, evangelical nationalism! On Martin Luther King Jr. weekend, the National March for Life was taking place in Washington DC. The March for Life is a protest march against abortion- a woman's right to choose for her own body. Thousands of demonstrators had paraded in the heart of Washington DC. protesting *Roe vs. Wade* calling for legal protections for unborn babies in the mother's womb.

Near the end of the protest, a group of Catholic high school students were waiting for their bus to pick them up. According to the initial narrative, a few students start a skirmish with a Native American elder, counter-protesting the march. Cameras start to roll as the confrontation appears to escalate between this old, wise Native-American Elder and these young catholic students wearing "Make America Great Again" red hats (in support of President Donald Trump). Things get really heated as the Native American elder are in confrontation with these young white, Anglo-saxon students. Still photos show an angry Native American Elder and a few smiling young white privileged students in "red hats".

In a rush to judgment, the two young catholic high school students found themselves caught in a national cultural firestorm. Celebrities and mainstream media outlets rushed to quickly condemn the students and the stereotype them as examples of the whole pro-Trump, evangelical, anti-abortion, homophobic, Islamaphobic, anti-progress nationalist "camp": white privileged, arrogant, narrow-minded, and using their position of white privilege to oppress a historically disenfranchised people group in the United States. Consider the following statements:

This is a disgrace. This is not America.

10

Let's not forget—this entire event happened because a group of boys went on a school-sanctioned trip to protest against a woman's right to her own body and reproductive healthcare. It is not debatable that bigotry was there right from the start- Alyssa Milano 1/21/2019

Other reactions on social media are not even re-printable. The intention of the limited video and still photos: to extol the virtues of pluralistic, progressive globalism and condemn dangerous nationalism. However, was this *the whole truth?*

The date of the March for Life in Washington DC was also the date the very first indigenous peoples' march was also scheduled. Later video surfaced showing a group called the Hebrew Israelites shouting slurs against Native Americans that were also marching that day. The four African American Hebrew Israelites then started peppering the students from Covington Highschool with insults as they were waiting for their buses. Attempting to drown out the hateful message, of the Hebrew Israelites, the students began a school chant that was okayed by the school chaperones.

This loud chanting was then misinterpreted as an aggressive angry white mob by the Native American leader, Nathan Philips. Fearful that they may retaliate against the Hebrew Israelites, Philips then attempted to intervene and got in front of the young Covington high school students. It was here where the historic picture and short video clips show what appears to be mocking and smug quiet smiles by the young Covington High School students. Longer video clips show Covington High School students standing there, smiling, and refusing to further escalate a potentially explosive confrontation.

The buses then came to pick up the Covington High School students and that appeared to be the end of the story. Meanwhile, Nathan Philips turned to other Native American marchers signaling victory. How then, did a minor incident with no violence "blow up" into a national firestorm of controversy? We need to look back at President Obama's presidency and the 2016 U.S. Presidential election contest for clues.

Understanding Obama's presidency and the 2016 Presidential Election

To understand the 2016 Presidential election, we need to look at the presidency of Barak Obama. In 2008 a mild recession exploded into a complete economic crisis as the credit crunch exploded. The Dow Jones plunged 777.68 points when the United States Government refused to bail out creditors, letting them fail. The U.S. led global economic system appeared as if it was in jeopardy. Due in part to the economic crisis, Barak Obama was elected president of the United States.

Under the leadership of President Obama, progressive globalism took large steps forward. Under his leadership, the "affordable health care act" was passed requiring universal health care insurance for everyone-and offering it to everyone as well. Homosexual "civil unions" were okayed and then the U.S. Supreme Court legalized homosexual marriage in 2015- that Barak Obama advocated for. Greater dependency on globalism and multi-national corporations emerged under Barak Obama. The entire culture of the United States became much more secularized and globalized from 2009 to 2016.

However, perhaps President Obama tried to do too much to quickly in the arena of globalism. The Arab Spring of 2011 was intended to help prepare the way for humanistic democracy in the Middle East, but what emerged in Egypt was that Mohamed Morsi, an Islamic Jihadist, was then "popularly elected" in the aftermath- until the army staged a coup to return Egypt to more moderate, secular rule. Brexit exploded on to the scene as rural United Kingdom voted to exit the European Union-and overwhelmed the urban, upper-class vote to remain. (Of course, the execution of leaving the EU was left to the educated elite-who voted against leaving-imagine how this is going to turn out.)

The United States was also ready to change- while Wall Street was rebounding nicely to soar to unprecedented levels, Main Street was not necessarily following suit. Many good paying, manufacturing jobs had been shipped overseas to places like China, India, and other nations-only to be replaced by lower paying service or retailing jobs. As the result, many middle-class families were struggling more severely as they had not recovered from the recession. Globalism was viewed as working for "the cultural, political, and economic elites" of society, but not for mainstream America.

Into the vacuum came Donald Trump: a billionaire, brash, blunt-talking nationalist. His vision and campaign slogan: "Make America Great Again" or "America First". During the 2016 election, Donald Trump ran as a political outsider, not really affiliated with the Republican or Democratic party. Running as a Republican, no one gave Donald Trump much of a chance to win the primary, let alone the presidency. Most of the mainstream media coverage focused on the primary election between Hilary Clinton and Bernie Sanders. To the shock of many, Donald Trump won the Republican Nomination for President- offending many establishment Republicans-some of them who hold to an Americanized globalist dream.

The 2016 general election campaign turned downright nasty. During the general election campaign, both candidates and their supporters managed to baptize the other side in muck. Donald Trump managed to offend virtually every disenfranchised group of people according to the mainstream media: The LGBTQ community, the Islamic community, the Latino community with his goal to "build the wall" to stop illegal immigration from Mexico, the pro-choice community, the African American community, and many others. Meanwhile, Hilary Clinton labeled evangelical Christians and others white nationalists as a "basket of deplorables" during an infamous fundraising campaign speech. Major media outlets expected election night to be a cake walk for Hilary Clinton with some prognosticators predicting an electoral college blowout.

Even Donald Trump thought things would go "according to plan" as the night began. Hilary Clinton had rented out the main New York Convention center for a large, glitzy election returns party. Meanwhile, Donald Trump rented out a ballroom at the last minute- and the media was covering the contrast. CNN, MSNBC, and most other news outlets were excited to crown Hilary Clinton the first woman President in U.S. history.

Many of us watched how the night unfolded: first there was concern as Virginia was not called for Hilary Clinton early. Kentucky came in with a much larger margin of victory for Trump than expected. The first returns from Florida were much closer than expected. The excitement of the evening turned to anxiety over the unexpected election returns: Ohio was called for Donald Trump. Major news networks still expected Clinton to win, but now it was looking like a long night. Thankfully the "blue wall" of states that were more favorable to Hilary Clinton (Michigan, Wisconsin, Pennsylvania, and Minnesota) were expected to still secure the necessary electoral votes for Hilary Clinton to be elected President.

The anxiety turned to outright panic at roughly 10pm local time: Florida has gone to Donald Trump along with North Carolina and Iowa. Meanwhile the returns out of Michigan, Wisconsin, and Pennsylvania were extremely troubling as well: Donald Trump was ahead in these states-where pollsters confidently predicted a Clinton victory. A horrible reality check swept through most media outlets: Donald Trump could become the President of the United States of America.

Reaction was severe: Dow Jones Industrial Average futures dropped in excess of 700 points. The Canadian immigration website crashed from large numbers of inquiries. Shocked, sickened, and sad people began reacting to the increasing likelihood of a Trump Presidency. CNN, MSNBC, ABC struggled to describe the painful reality of the actual vote totals coming in: How had the polls missed this badly? Why was Hilary Clinton, the most qualified woman to be President in history, losing the election?

Donald Trump was carrying the white uneducated vote by more than 50 percentage points. Evangelical Christians flooded to the polls to vote for Donald Trump-or perhaps against Hilary Clinton's (and President Obama's) globalist, progressive policies. The gender gap (voting preferences between men and women) was not as large as Clinton had hoped for. The African American vote in the big industrial cities had not turned out for Hilary Clinton.

As the vote totals continued to come in, one CNN commentator described the event as "whitelash"- the white "majority" was rising up in nationalist racism to vote in favor of Donald Trump. Other commentators described the middle class revolting against the cultural elites in the media, government, marketplace, and entertainment industries. Still other social commentators struggled to keep their composure as at last the Presidential race was called: Trump had won the Presidential election.

The "basket of deplorables" had changed American politics. One CNN commentator probably got it right: the election was about globalism versus nationalism. Nationalism in the form of Donald Trump had become a formidable roadblock to progressive globalism within the United States of America. The incident involving the Covington Catholic High school students re-opened and highlighted the many deep offenses and emphasized the massive cultural divide in the United States of America. Can we define the problem? Is there a solution to the problem? The progressive left is pushing an ill-defined humanistic narrative that I will help them define in more concrete terms: "The Gospel of Globalism".

What is the Gospel of Globalism?

The word "gospel" literally means good news. Typically, this word has been used in Christian circles describing what the Bible says about Jesus Christ. However, the term can be applied to any narrative that exposes a deep existential problem and proposes a wonderful solution. A gospel narrative ends with the proposed solution effectively solving the problem resulting in peace and joy for those who were faithful to the narrative message. The Bible warns against receiving a false (or alternative) gospel many times.

Yet in bits and pieces, we can perceive an alternative "gospel" narrative emerging: The Gospel of Globalism. Media outlets such as CNN and MSNBC are touting the virtue of globalism, open borders, free health care for everyone, tolerance, and moral relativism along with the depravity of "backward thinking" nationalists, the problems of lack of social injustice, and old entrenched belief systems. Key unanswered questions are: What is the end-goal agenda of this globalism "gospel" narrative? How is globalism supposed to bring peace and joy to the whole earth?

As we approach the 2020 presidential election, the United States remains deeply divided between Progressive globalists and Nationalists. What makes progressive globalism so good and grand? Conspiracy theorists tout the evil of the "New World Order" and the threat of globalist government. Progressive globalists tout the problem of old inferior belief systems to as a barrier to progress and prosperity and characterize President Donald Trump as a prime example of this terrible problem. What is the underlying worldview behind the cultural values of progressive globalism? What is the ultimate end-goal for progressive globalists? In order to understand the roots of the Gospel of Globalism and the cultural divide in the United States, we must first turn to the history of the United States and key advancements of science/technology from around the world.

Chapter 2: The roots of Nationalism in the United States of America.

To understand this globalist gospel narrative, we need to understand American history. Christopher Columbus discovered the continent of North America in 1492. However, it is clear from the ruins of the Mayans and the Aztecs that people had been inhabiting North and South America far earlier than this. The Bible describes "the earth" ("the land" in Hebrew) being divided (Genesis 10:25) in the days of Peleg.

Fast forward to 1607 with the first settlers coming in ships Jamestown Colony under Rev. James Black came ashore from England. Rev. James Black dedicated the land to the glory of God, the spread of the gospel of Jesus Christ and speeding forward the return of Jesus. Shortly thereafter, the more famous English settlement in Plymouth, Massachusetts was established-the pilgrims. They were Puritans seeking relief from religious persecution and freedom to worship God. They were going to a land they would later name "New England".

The Puritan colonies are most remembered for "the first Thanksgiving" where the Puritans and Indians celebrated a friendship feast together. The Puritan colony faced a very hard winter where many starved to death after they had problems getting crops to grow. It was a famous Native American named Squanto who helped the first English settlers acclimate to the land: what crops would grow, how to hunt for food, various native plants that could be used for food or other purposes, and other survival skills in this large new land. To understand what really helped shaped "classic nationalism" in America, we need to understand the life and values of these first settlers.

18

The land, the first settlers, and their worldview values.

The new land was very harsh and unforgiving. There were no inter-state highways to make travel fast and easy. If you were hungry or needed something, you could not simply get in the car and drive down to Walmart to go get it. There was no modern medicine if you became seriously ill. Rivers were crucial for both travel, commerce, and for providing fertile land. It took weeks or months for "current events" to cross the frontier. All this helped fashion and form the first cultural values of this "new world" and its puritan settlers that shaped United States, American culture.

Within this vast and new land, there were also many life-and-death challenges. First, there was the issue of gathering or growing food: what grows in the soil of the new land? Were there native plants that were good for food? What about native plants that were poisonous? Were there animals that could be hunted for food or for their skins to help stay warm? Were there animals that were dangerous such as bears, wolves, or other predators that could kill someone and end the frontier dream? What about hidden diseases in the land? Then there was the question of native tribes or people groups in the land: Were they friendly? Where they hostile? How could the new settlers negotiate with these small tribes in the land? The new land provided for many dangerous challenges and survival was difficult.

The Puritans were very religious- in that they had the fear of God as part of their worldview. Either God needed to help them settle the new, hostile land or they would die. The Puritans believed if the community tolerated sin according to the Bible, God would punish them severely by sending famine or pestilence. Therefore, community punishments including "branding", being put in the stocks, and even hanging were possible for things such as adultery, sexual immorality, or taking the Lord's name in vain. Classic fiction such as *The Scarlet Letter* detail some of the community punishments for certain "crimes" against the society.

Their religious background encouraged hard work as part of their worship to God. (Even some of the Greek biblical words for worship are the same as work.) The Puritans believed the laziness was serious sin and greatly frowned upon. Therefore, they encouraged a vigorous work ethic to "get the job done". Often, getting the job done meant the difference between survival and relative prosperity (above what their neighbor was able to do) or it meant begging for help, indentured servitude, or even worse-starving to death in the harsh winter with snow and cold.

Due to the remoteness of the land, it was every community for themselves in this vast new land. Communal farms had been tried, but they turned into a disaster. Rugged individualism was encouraged and community lands were divided-meaning it was every man/household for themselves. There were no taxes or oppression by foreign governments. While life was very difficult in this new land, at least the people had religious freedom and the possibility of a better life.

There was also the excitement of pioneering something new: There is always the sense of adventure of trying to accomplish something never been done before. The first settlers had a dream for their children: Perhaps through their hard work and perseverance, they could begin building a home that their children and grandchildren would live grow up better off. There was always the dream that future generations in the land might have a better life because of the sacrifice of the first pioneering settlers. As the result, the parents sacrificed with the hope of their children getting a better life.

The first Great Awakening reinforced many of these values and made them personal. In 1741, Jonathan Edwards preached the now famous message "Sinners in the Hands of an Angry God" causing a massive personal response. This helped spark a renewal of Christian enthusiasm and personal conversion experiences by the tens of thousands across the newly settled land. There were other revivals that preached throughout Europe around this time as well.

This first great awakening also helped reinforce some of the original values: the fear of the Lord and freedom to worship God as they saw fit without the threat of persecution, the puritan work ethic, and a desire to leave an inheritance to their children and grandchildren. These biblical values were worth fighting for and this led to division among denominations- some wanted nothing to do with this new "religious enthusiasm" while others openly embraced this. As this great awakening was affecting the culture of colonial society, so it was also causing division over the future of the colonies. What united the Colonies was the fear of God- many of our earliest mottos focus on "One Nation under God" or "In God we trust".

The need for more organized government while avoiding oppressive tyranny.

The first colonist settlers of the 1600's eventually formed small communities-which in turn formed into larger communities as more settlers came in from overseas and the English colonists eventually had offspring. More organized forms of government needed to be set in place as the number of people in the colonies was increasing. All this was happening as the influence of the first great spiritual awakening was erupting into the conscience of society.

In addition, with the increasing population came increasing productivity and profits- and the motherland, England wanted to share in the profits of its territory across the sea. The English monarchy wanted more economic tribute and governmental control from the emerging colonies along the east coast of the United States. This led to increasing tensions between some of the Colonists and the English Crown and control.

The Colonies were not recognized as having a voice before the English crown- but they were "conquered territory" where

English settlers (presumed loyal to the crown) were to reap the benefits of the land and then share the resources with English headquarters in London. In protests some of the colonists destroyed a whole shipment of tea by throwing it into Boston Harbor. Taxation without representation became the rallying cry for a revolution-causing division. Some of the settlers were loyalists to the British crown. Others wanted revolution. Many stayed neutral and wanted to see "what happened".

The tensions continued to grow until July 4th, 1776 when the declaration of Independence was signed by Colonist leaders in Philadelphia, Pennsylvania. Those who signed the declaration of Independence knew they were putting life and property at risk. If their bid for independence failed, they would be publicly humiliated, tortured, and then executed by the British monarchy. Meanwhile, the British Crown was not about to let a significant source of income suddenly dry up-and they responded accordingly. With the first shots at Lexington and Concord in 1775, the U.S. Revolutionary war began.

It was a military mismatch between the world's strongest military (the British Army and Navy) and a bunch of Colonists with a loosely formed militia. There was a time where the sun never set on the British empire-the dominant superpower of the day. The British military were the first ones to have cannons. George Washington lost more battles than he won to the British-and had to spend a very difficult winter with the troops at Valley Forge- where many died. While at Valley Forge, George Washington had a strange encounter or vision which indicated that he would get victory that is recorded in the Library of Congress. For some reason and against all-odds, General George Washington ended up leading continental army to victory over the British with the decisive victory coming at Yorktown with an assist to the French Navy. The British left leaving the colonies independent- now what?

Officially forming a new government

After the British left and the euphoria of defeating the British ended there was now a huge problem: How do we prevent this tyranny again? Great minds such as John Hamilton, Thomas Jefferson, and others wrote *The Federalist Papers* detailing the underlying philosophy of how the new government should be formed. The theology of the day emphasized the deep depravity of humanity and the tendency for humans in power to become tyrants. Much denominational theology taught about the "total depravity of man" where human sin was actually- the underlying cause of all tyranny. Only God could change the heart of men to remove the deep wicked tendency for human beings to oppress other human beings.

With the seeds of tyranny and oppression in the hearts of people, what could be done to effectively govern a nation? The values of individual freedom and keeping order in society often contradicted each other in forming both philosophy and policy. There was the danger of the tyranny of the minority: The colonists had learned from the experience of "taxation without representation" that had fueled the revolutionary war with England. However, there was also the danger of "the tyranny of the majority" where the majority would pass laws to oppress the minority they didn't agree with. The number of tyrannical incidents of injustice meted out by the majority was becoming significant, with the Salem Witch Trials a well-known example.

The Salem Witch trials in the 1690's showed our founding fathers the danger of "tyranny of the majority" leading to accusations of heinous evil, dehumanization of the accused, and then execution of undesirables based on heresy, and a breakdown of the justice system. As the result of rumors, and the lack of physical or eyewitness evidence, roughly 20 people were convicted of practicing witchcraft (a capital offense in the Puritan community) on rather questionable evidence, and then put to death.

In the end, the founding fathers wrote the U.S. Constitution and divided the government into three parts: The Legislative branch that would write the laws of the land, the Judicial branch which was critical to interpreting and applying the laws of the land, the Executive Branch would enforce the laws of the land. With the division of the government came a separation of powers along with a system of checks and balances: Why?

While most believed only God could stop tyranny in the human heart, it was up to men to defend freedom and turn back oppressors from controlling all the people. "The Government by the people and for the people" was designed to detect, challenge, and eliminate Tyranny that might raise its ugly head in the newly formed government. The government was also to represent the interests of the people. The underlying values of this new fledgling nation would be: the fear of God, independence and political freedom, hard work, and a hope that successive generations would have better lives than the parents had. In 1791, the Constitution was ratified by the states and a new nation was formed: The United States of America.

Chapter 3: A history of achievements and misdeeds

In 1791, a new nation was officially formed: The United States of America. Westward expansion was beginning but there were still many challenges related founding a nation. Other European nations such as France, England, and Spain still had land interests in "the new world". There was also the issue of relating to Native American tribes such as the Dakota Sioux, the Navajo, and Apache. The land was raw and needed to be subdued and developed with threats such as droughts, floods, severe storms, extreme heat, harsh winters, and other hazards such as hostile wildlife and disease outbreaks.

Napoleon's offer that was too good to refuse

Only 12 years later, Napoleon of France offered a wonderful land deal- the newly formed United States could purchase land rights encompassing a large chunk of the continent for a nominal price: the cancelation of French debts and a few million dollars. With this great land deal, France was also offering friendship with the United States for continued trade purposes. The U.S. government then commissioned Meriwether Lewis and William Clark to explore and map the new territory. The "Lewis and Clark" expedition became part of American folklore, and helped to strengthen the forerunner, pioneering spirit within the United States.

Of course, Napoleon had his own globalist ambitions: He needed finances to fund his own political and military ambitions in Europe. The land purchased from France allowed Napoleon to raise up powerful armies to sweep across Europe and France became a mighty empire that threatened the political sovereignty of England and other European nations. In England's view, the newly formed United States had helped to create a huge problem in Europe with the Louisiana purchase.

As the result, the threat of Napoleonic France to England stirred up tensions between the newly formed United States and England again. A few more skirmishes provoked another war with the United States. Hostilities broke out again in 1812 including battles on the land. A strange tornado stopped the British from advancing upon and taking over the newly built Washington DC capital of the United States-after they had apparently won a decisive battle. The United States called it Divine providence. The British decided that invading and conquering the United States was virtually impossible due to the large amount of undeveloped territory the United States and the ongoing threat of Napoleon to the homeland of England.

On the other side of the ocean, Russia was forced to defend itself against Napoleon's invasion. To commemorate the event, Peter Tchaikovsky wrote the 1812 Overture with its finale of canon fire and church bells. When he then toured the United States, the 1812 Overture became an American favorite since the United States had just defended itself against the attempts of the British to take over the United States.

With the Louisiana Purchase and the successful defense against the British in the war of 1812, the newly formed United States was the dominant nation in the new (mostly unexplored) continent of North America. People across Europe were invited to come immigrate after Napoleon lost. There were vast new tracts of untamed farmland and wilderness. There was the promise of religious freedom (within Christianity) as sectarianism was a significant issue in Europe. Through the values of hard work (puritan work ethic), the fear of God with religious devotion, freedom to pursue life, liberty and happiness, and the dream of children and grandchildren having a much better life; the nation was gradually being settled and expanded.

As the result of freedom of religion, freedom of expression and speech, along with freedom of "life, liberty and the pursuit of happiness", the newly formed United States became a hotbed for new extraordinary inventions. Thomas Edison invented light-bulbs in the 1800's. Mr. Goodyear invented vulcanized rubber. Many other inventions that formed the foundation of modern society came from American soil in the 1800's. All of these new inventions enabled the United States to produce great wealth for future generations.

Misdeed: "Manifest destiny" and Native Americans.

However, things were not rosy for everyone. As westward expansion continued, the view of Native Americans such as the Sioux, the Apache, and the Chippewa spiraled downward. They were looked down upon and viewed as "savages" by the white, Anglo-Saxon, Protestants with their primitive housing, nomadic lifestyle, and esoteric spirituality. The worldview clash between White Anglo-Saxon protestants and many Native American spiritual practices often spilled over into violence and bloodshed.

As the result, on the early 1800's Native American Nations such as the Cherokee, Seminole, and Chickasaw were removed from the Southeast and forced westward to "Indian Territory" (now known as Oklahoma). Treaty after treaty was broken by the Federal Government in the name of "progress" and "might makes right". In this forced march from the Southeastern United States, many Native Americans perished along what became known as "The Trail of Tears".

Beginning after the 1849 goldrush to California, expansion westward accelerated. There was much more opportunity to be explored. The great westward expansion continued as much of the United States of America adopted the doctrine of "Manifest Destiny"- coined by John O Sullivan in 1845. It was the belief system that the United States was destined to conquer the new territory and spread virtues of Protestantism and freedom to the entire North American Continent.

Theological justification came from Joshua and the children of Israel's conquest of Canaan and the heathen nations that possessed the land. Since the theology of the time viewed the Church as "the New Israel", there was a divine mandate to conquer the territory, Christianize it and expand the prosperity that was already occurring in places already settled. There were nations such as the Sioux, the Chippewa, the Cherokees, and Apache that kept idolatrous evil religious practices for generations and the white settlers were viewed as instruments of God to bring either salvation for these nations from such evil practices- or judgment for refusing to change. The end objectives of "manifest destiny" justified the means- even if it meant breaking hundreds of treaties with Native American nations.

As the result of broken treaties, trust was obliterated between the U.S. Federal government and Native American tribes. Bloody skirmishes and warfare continued through the 1800's as Native American Tribes fought to preserve their land and way of life. However, numerically, there was no chance for these Native American Tribes to hold out against the increasing number of settlers due to immigration, families having children and grandchildren, and increasingly technologically advanced weapons. As the result, Many Native Americans nations were virtually exterminated, forced on to reservations or forcefully assimilated at boarding schools (located in places such as Canton, South Dakota and Lawrence, Kansas). In the name of "liberty and justice for all", this conquest quite often produced the opposite.

Misdeed: African American Slavery and the civil war.

Even among those who embraced "Manifest Destiny" there was division: Some believed the enslavement of African Americans was justified in the Bible and practically: After all, African Americans had been taken out of Africa where barbaric tribal practices included black magick, idolatry, and tribalistic warfare. At least under the slavery influence of Europeans, they had the ability to hear about the gospel according to Protestantism.

Others from the north believed that Slavery of African Americans was completely wrong in every way and were willing to fight for it. Harriett Beecher Stowe's novel *Uncle Tom's Cabin* exposed the underbelly of the horrific practices associated with African American Slavery: There were horrific decisions like Dred Scott that ruled that an African slave7 was not really a human being, but property that could be bought and sold. There were the horrific passages to America aboard slave ships across the Atlantic where African American were treated like cattle. African American families were split apart on the auction blocks in places like St. Augustine in the name of greed, and profits. There were the horrible beatings and cruel punishments associated with disobedience or slaves attempting to escape. Females were forced into breeding of African Americans into slavery. This injustice was so severe that it was willing to fight over- to prevent the expansion of this atrocity.

The fight started in the politics of the day: The southern states that were promoting slavery needed to be kept in check politically- if more slave states were admitted into the union than states favoring the abolition of slavery; the "slave states" would have the majority and be able to pass legislation allowing slavery in the entire United States of America. A rush to bring "free states" into the Union came in during the 1840's and 1850's. This brought bloody clashes in Missouri and Kansas. Anti-slavery states were winning the political battle of the day causing the Southern states to talk about a different solution: secession and division of the union.

Due to backward thinking that justified slavery that was so ingrained in the culture, the result was devastating. When Abraham Lincoln, an overt abolitionist, was elected president from Illinois, this was the last straw- The Executive Branch combined with the Legislative branch was going to oppress and force abolition on the South along with destroying the antebellum culture in the southern states. For many in the south, this way of life in the south was worth fighting for-even if it meant dividing up the United States of America.

The fight began innocuously when Fort Sumpter was attacked in April, 1961. It was a spectacular scene but signaled to the northern Union States that the new Southern Confederacy was really serious about their intent to divide the union. At the 70-year mark, The United States was facing a fight to survive as one nation. The North was going to war to preserve the Union (some of the Union States permitted slavery). Thus began a destructive civil war that cost hundreds of thousands of lives, untold suffering (especially across the south), and the first war where civilian facilities became targets as the whole population was viewed as involved in the war effort through the production of resources used for warfare.

In the midst of the civil war, Abraham Lincoln gave the famous "Emancipation Proclamation" announcing freedom for all slaves in the south and basically outlawing slavery when the Union was restored. The Union states of the North were strategically superior to the South in terms population, and ability to produce weapons and other resources needed to wage war. However, how much would this war cost in terms of suffering? Abraham Lincoln believed that slavery had caused the judgment of God to come to the nation in the form of the Civil War- and stated such in his 2nd inaugural address.

The war ended on April 9th, 1865 at Appomattox courthouse with over 600,000 dead, and many others suffering. In the midst of the war, Abraham Lincoln worked hard to diffuse bitterness, not "demonize the south", and seeking "malice towards none" that would have opened the doors for continued bitterness, vengeance, and oppression against those who had caused the war. The final terms of surrender were incredibly generous: The soldiers of the south would not be imprisoned or tried for treason. If they simply laid down their weapons of war, they were free to return home and get on with helping their families and their communities put food on the table.

Why was the war over with victory for the north and mercy leading to reconciliation for the south? Abraham Lincoln believed that God was very angry over slavery and the terrible war was a corporate judgment of God for shedding blood associated with the systematic injustice of slavery. In the Bible, destructive war and captivity was a judgment from God for idolatry and systematic injustice- like what was happening in Israel according to the prophet Jeremiah. There were virtually no open secular humanists or atheists in the culture at that time to offer a counter-argument: Was it simply the perseverance of the human spirit? Did the union simply survive by chance?

In any case, after the war ended, both the northern states and the southern states could agree: "Never Again!" A truly united, United States of America could get on with expanding liberty and freedom across the North American Continent for everyone- including African Americans (and maybe Native Americans). The brutality of the civil war helped shaped American understanding of social justice- the need to help the oppressed and poor. Is this in the Bible or human sympathy- a forerunner to the globalism "gospel" narrative?

Chapter 4: The United States enters the Global scene in the 20th century

At the turn of the 20th century, the United States had basically finished westward expansion and reached the Pacific Ocean. The freedom of speech, freedom to worship, and liberty backed up by the right to bear arms allowed creativity and exploration to flourish. Many new inventions had come from the United States in the 19th and early 20th century such as the airplane, radio broadcast, and the assembly line. The impacts of these inventions could not fully be appreciated for another few decades, but they would have huge implications for the future of the United States and beyond.

However, on the global scene the United States was still quite isolated from the rest of the world. There was no television or internet, so news still traveled slowly across the United States via the U.S. postal service, newspapers, and town-criers. The news sometimes took weeks to arrive. News from overseas could take weeks or months to arrive. Broadcast technology (such as radio) was still in its infancy. The North American Continent was still isolated away from what was still viewed as the center of Western Civilization: Europe. Other large civilizations existed in Asia (China and India), and Africa. However, there were even larger difficulties for receiving news from these parts of the earth.

When the Archduke of Austria was assassinated, it brought Austria and Serbia into conflict that simmered for a short time as news of this terrible event eventually spread across Europe. Austria eventually responded to the assassination by attacking Serbia's capital. This mobilized Russia behind Serbia. Behind Austria was Germany and other nations. Behind Serbia was Russia, France, and England in a military alliance. The war was on!

In the midst of the great war to "end all wars", the United States remained neutral. However, due to geography, the United States traded with France and England more than Germany allowing supplies to come from the United States to help their side of the fight. Germany understood this and Germany attacked the United States shipping and tried to incite Mexico to enter the war on Germany's side. This brought the United States into the war formally against the Germans and implicitly against the Austrians and Italy. Millions of U.S. troops poured into Europe, just as the war was beginning to wind down. Eventually a series of peace treaties were signed ending the war, but they left Germany under harsh restrictions after the war. The United States was now being taken seriously as a world power-but the world still revolved around Europe.

The 1920's saw a booming United States economy. Known as the "roaring 20's" the stock-market went on roughly a decade-long upward trend. All of the innovation and technology helped to fuel record production and change practical life with new technology in the homes such as electrical lighting. Expectations of greater things to come were at an all-time high, fueling the economic speculation. Symbolic of the booming U.S. economy of the "roaring 20's". the iconic Empire State Building was actually completed as the "booming economy" went bust in 1930-1931.

'The Greatest Generation'

With the sudden stock market crash in October 1929, this optimistic worldview came crashing down along with the profits on Wall Street. News spread much faster with the advent of Radio News programs in the 1920's. Eventually the losses on paper (due to the stock market crash) from Wall Street began to negatively affect the practical day-to-day economics on Main Street. Multitudes of banks failed causing families to lose their hard-earned inheritances by the thousands. Unemployment skyrocketed as fear and pessimistic prognostications dominated economic outlooks.

The stock market crash led to a global economic depression. Even back in the 1930's the economies of the world were becoming more interconnected. The United States backed off importing foreign goods with the goal of stimulating U.S. manufacturing jobs. However, other nations were also buying fewer American goods as well, deepening the depression in the United States. At the height of the economic depression, the unemployment rate hit 25% and another 25% or so were under-employed.

In the United States, a generation of children grew up in the 1910's and 1920's in an era of innocence and overwhelming optimism. Then the 1929 stock market crash and optimism hit the wall of reality. These children were now teenagers and young adults in the 1930's and facing a very uncertain future. How would a whole generation respond? Was it time to launch a political revolution like in other nations? Like 70 years prior, the United States of America was facing a profound crisis economic and political crisis. A new deal helped the youth of the United States to scrap ideas of a revolution- and brought massive governmental expansion.

The United States was not alone in suffering from the great depression. The economic depression deeply hit Germany as well. National pride had been shattered after World War I and the treaties signed deeply restricted Germany's economic engine and military. This led to political instability in the nation as the German people were tired of the oppressive status quo. Into this void stepped a corporal from Austria, a governmental agitator named Adolf Hitler.

Using a series of shrewd political maneuvers and threats of brute force, Hitler muscled himself to the top of the German government. Hitler and the Nazi party blamed the Jewish people for all of Germany's problems. His oratorial skill swept the German people off their feet, and a most of the German people were hoodwinked at his personal charisma and his ability to deliver on his promises that seemed impossible. Perhaps Adolf Hitler would lead

Germany out of its economic and emotional depression and back into nationalistic glory.

However, he had ambitions beyond simply making Germany great again. He was a governmental agitator and Hitler's intention was to agitate the balance of power throughout Europe. Instead of focusing on domestic relief, he focused on rebuilding the military, beyond what was permitted after World War I. He remilitarized the Rhineland. The emphasis on military spending and ambition re-ignited Germany's economy. In response to these aggressive, agitating moves, Italy, France, and Great Britain did nothing as these nations were also suffering from the Great Depression and were ill-prepared for war in the early to mid-1930's.

Finally, the breakout of war was inevitable. Germany invaded Poland, justifying this aggressive action by accusing the Polish of attacking Germany first in a few minor skirmishes. France and England declared war but were quite unprepared for the German onslaught. By the end of 1940 it appeared that Germany was on the verge of taking over all of Europe. Only a miracle saved the British army from annihilation on France's shores.

Meanwhile, the Anti-Semitism that was at the foundation of Germany's governmental philosophy was now openly manifest. Millions of Jews were being taken in trains to relocation concentration camps where they were worked to death, experimented on, or executed. A great evil had enveloped all of Europe as Hitler's Germany had ambitions to become the dominant power in all of the earth along with the axis alliance in Italy and Japan along with other nations who supported Germany's Anti-Semetism.

While the United States was a growing economic power with its manufacturing abilities and inventions, the United States attempted to remain neutral (again) in the midst of the war in Europe and Asia. This changed on December 7th, 1941 when the

Japanese attacked Pearl Harbor, awakening a whole generation to the great danger against liberty. Out of anger for being blind-sided and in zeal to protect freedom, the nation was mobilized to set Europe free from the extreme right-wing danger represented by Adolf Hitler. Finally, in 1945, Germany surrendered followed quickly by Japan ending World War II. The Allies of England, France, the United States and Russia were victorious.

In the midst of the Allied victory, there was still turmoil and danger. There were growing reports of the danger that Stalin's communism was posing to the world. Joseph Stalin had killed or imprisoned millions of his own people who disagreed with his communistic philosophy. There were reports at how Russia had basically annexed Poland in the wake of World War II. What if Stalin had global ambitions like Adolf Hitler? Even during World War II there was a race to get new "super weapons".

Meanwhile in the aftermath of World War II, more than 50 million people were dead. Much of Europe and parts of Asia were devastated and needed to be rebuilt. The people of Europe were still facing massive suffering and even starvation as the infrastructure in the nations had been decimated. Instead of the United States occupying Germany and Japan to oppress them, (as most victorious empires had) the United States did something unusual- they helped rebuild their infrastructure, bring relief to the people, and restore responsible self-government by the people without oppression. The threat of communism taking over Europe strengthened the resolve of the United States and Allies to help their former Axis enemies.

The United States had demonstrated the power of splitting an atom over Japan and the nations of the earth were now horrified at the human toll the next war could cause upon humanity. There was a growing danger of humanity collectively committing suicide through starting another major war. Above national governments, something greater was needed to help prevent another World War. As the result, the United Nations was born as a first, very loose attempt at global government. It's one main function to begin with was simply to prevent World War III.

Meanwhile the same generation who had their hopes shattered in the stock market crash in 1920's lived through the depression and adversity of the 1930's were now the young people who faced the extreme adversity in World War II. These were now the same more mature people who helped rebuild Europe to help protect Europe from the new threat of tyranny on the left in the form of atheistic Communism. Journalist Tom Brokaw named this generation "the Greatest Generation" in 1998.

Post- World War II challenges:

World War II redrew the global political map. Word spread to the rest of the world through theatres about the atrocities committed against the Jews under Nazi Germany in World War II. Over 6 million Jews were exterminated. Under Harry S. Truman, the United States was determined to give the Jewish people a homeland. Through a series of strong-armed political maneuvers and global sympathy, on May 14th, 1948 the state of Israel was born enraging many Islam-dominated nations that immediately declared war. Over the next several decades, Islamic dominated nations attempted to attack Israel several times, each time failing against all odds.

Communism was growing into a global threat. Communist Russia acquired nuclear weapons. In 1949 the Communist party launched the cultural revolution that transformed the nation of China into a Communist nation. Under Chairman Mao, millions of people were killed. The Communists took over North Korea resulting in overwhelming suffering and a war that left the Korean peninsula devastated. Communist ideology swept through many of the "stan" nations in Eurasia that became united under the banner of the United Soviet Socialist Republics (U.S.S.R.). Other nations such as Poland, the Romania, and the Slavic nations were intimidated into joining the Soviet Bloc. The U.S.S.R seemed poised to invade western

Europe and spread "godless communism" and tyranny across the world. Who could stop them?

The United States had only reluctantly entered World War II. However, such a policy could not be repeated with Communism as devastating weapons were being developed that could strike the United States from half-way around the world. The United States was asked to keep the balance in Europe. The resulting political, economic, religious, and military stand-off in Europe became known as "The Cold War" between the Christianized West and Atheistic Communism. Several times over the next decades, "the cold war" came to the brink of an actual war involving nuclear warfare. Would humanity extinguish itself through all-out nuclear war?

Meanwhile the political freedom environment, inventions of previous decades, and the confiscated German engineering plans allowed the United States to keep the edge economically. In the decades following the war, the United States became increasingly wealthy with technological innovations such as television, widespread use of automobiles, and air travel. The United States and the west would prove the superiority of democratic freedom and capitalism over Communistic philosophy economically. If the U.S.S.R. were to launch a man into space, the United States would be the first nation to place a man on the moon.

In 1985 a reformer named Mikhail Gorbachev became the head of state for the U.S.S.R. In 1987 (roughly 70 years after the communist revolution began), President Ronald Reagan addressed Mr. Gorbachev head-on at the Brandenburg Gate at the Berlin Wall: "Mr. Gorbachev, open this gate! Mr. Gorbachev, tear down this wall!" Two years later, a prayer meeting in East Germany ballooned into massive prayerful protests with candles. Earlier that same year, despite the best attempts to stymie the news by the Chinese communists, the depravity of China's government was on full display. Hundreds or thousands of protesters were killed around the Tianamen Square protests in Beijing in a government crackdown. Did

40

the communist East Germans want this to happen again in their nation with cameras rolling and the world watching?

By now, we all know the end of this story. In 1989, the Berlin Wall collapsed and with it the whole Eastern Bloc of nations. Mr. Gorbachev was not going to send in tanks and troops to hold on to communist territory like what had happened in Czechoslovakia. The United States had won the stand-off through superior economics. The United States was the sole political super-power, leading through influence and provoking other nations to follow us.

The Exaltation of the United States: Why?

The United States had become the dominant political, military, and economic power in the globe by 1990. Operation Desert Storm displayed this as the U.S. crushed Iraq's military for invading Kuwait. The key question is why?

Biblical Christians believe it was the godly foundations of our liberty: The fear of the Lord, hard work and sacrifice, and vision for the next generation to be better off than the previous one. Christians historians believe that it was God that allowed a generation to suffer deeply from shattered expectations and economic depression to be ready for the adversity of World War II to stop wickedness in the form of Nazi Germany. The United States did not like war, but when forced to take part in war, the United States was fighting to liberate the people from oppression and tyranny- a biblical value.

Many Christians also believe the United States has a sovereign purpose related to bringing the Gospel of the Kingdom to the ends of the earth and ushering in the return of Jesus. We know the United States was the first nation to recognize Israel as a nation and as the result were the recipients of the promised blessing in Genesis 12:1-3. Another reason relates to the Great Commission: Ministries such as Billy Graham, YWAM, and Every Home for Christ had a global impact to forcefully thrust the great commission to the ends of the earth.

Meanwhile, the globalist, humanistic narrative declares that it was due to human ingenuity, capitalism, and in the environment of political freedom and opportunity that made the difference. Great scientific inventions came forth from the United States that enabled the United States to be technologically superior to other nations such as Germany, the U.S.S.R, and other tyrannical leaders. Great strides have been made to remove discrimination against disadvantaged ethnic groups and hatred for lifestyles that are not viewed as "kosher". Thus, economic and political opportunity should be available to every person on the earth to see how much humanity can achieve without political or moral hindrance.

On September 11th, 2001 everything changed again when 19 terrorists destroyed the World Trade Center in New York City and attacked Washington DC. Almost 3,000 people were killed on that day and many more died prematurely due to the pollution caused by the World Trade Center attacks. The United States declared a "war on terror". The September 11th attacks affected everything- a whole generation has grown up in the shadow of 9-11. A whole generation is also growing up with new technological realities. To understand the Gospel of Globalism, we must look at the evolution of technological breakthroughs as well as some general cultural realities.

Chapter 5: The Travel and Digital revolution

In attempting to understand the secular Gospel of Globalism narrative, we need to look at the current status of society that has been generally fueled by technological revolution and critical inventions related to travel and communication.

Until the 20th century, life was primarily based on agriculture and building farmsteads to settle on. If it was a year of plenty, there was much rejoicing and celebration. If bad weather had robbed people of wheat and other food supplies, a barbaric winter was not something to look forward to. Would the grain or other staples last through the winter? If people survived the winter, spring brought fresh hope for a new and better crop. Eventually some settlements turned into cities on the frontier of America and became centers of commerce and production.

The travel revolution

The main mode of transportation locally was still by horse. Horse thievery was viewed as a very serious offense. However, horses could not be used long-distance over land easily as they required food, shelter, and adequate upkeep. Long distance travel time over land was very limited due to the requirement to take care of horses along with the necessity of taking care of supplies. A journey across the frontier with horses or oxen took weeks-documented through journals of travelers heading west to settle the new frontier as part of the great adventure.

Meanwhile, if someone wanted to go overseas, this was going to be a challenging and difficult voyage lasting weeks or months with great dangers of storms, running out of food, and disease etc. Taking on a long voyage across the ocean was to risk your life. Long-distance travel almost never happened-unless it was quite an emergency or seeking political or religious freedom. There were basically no vacations and very little leisure time.

Near the middle of the 20th century, there was a breakthrough in continental travel: railroad. In 1860 the first trans-continental railroad was built linking the Midwest to the west coast. Soon the rail-lines crossed the American frontier and long-distance travel time across land dropped from weeks to merely days. The pace of society sped up. News traveled across the country in days instead of weeks via town-criers.

The next breakthrough in transportation came in the early 20th century form of the assembly line, mass-production and this led to the advent of widespread use of the automobile. A German inventor invented the "motor wagon" in the 1880's, but they were very difficult and time-consuming to manufacture. With the advent of mass production, standardized parts, and the assembly line, production increased dramatically. Since then cars and then trucks became commonly used in the United States and Europe beginning in the 1920's and 1930's. Motor vehicles have become almost a necessity to function effectively in western society. The U.S. interstate system built by Dwight D. Eisenhower provided a grid of highways for motorists to quickly travel across the United States. Other nations such as China and the European Union built or rebuilt their road infrastructure. Travel times dropped again as local trips around the town or region dropped again. This caused the pace of society to speed up even farther.

The final breakthrough in transportation that shapes today's society was the advent of flight and airplanes in 1903 by the Wright brothers. Airplane technology was primarily researched and used by military in World War I and then in World War II. Jet propulsion was patented in 1930 and first used in warfare by the Germans near the end of WWII. Commercial air-travel became more common in the 1950's (even though it was primarily for the wealthier classes).

Traveling via airplane used to be a clear status symbol of wealth. As airplanes became more fuel efficient, the cost of air travel dropped as well. The advent of airplanes and affordable air travel has dropped global travel times further. Traveling overseas took weeks to accomplish a century ago. Today, a supersonic flight between New York City and London can be accomplished in roughly 6 hours. Air travel to virtually any part of the globe can be accomplished within 24 hours.

Commercial air travel has become common with international airports connecting virtually every geo-political nation together. Over 2.5 million people fly in the United States daily[1]. Hundreds of thousands more fly across the nations world-wide. Long-distance travel was viewed as very dangerous before the 20th century with many hazards associated with sailing by ships or travel by land. Today, virtually all flights safely make it to their destination- any rare commercial airplane crash quickly makes global headlines.

Global communication history

In 2019, it is now possible to travel across the sea to virtually any geo-political nation within 3 days where such a journey would have taken months or years in 1919. However, global communication is much quicker than this due to another revolution that has occurred in communication. The digital communication revolution is a fifth-generation communication breakthrough. We also need to understand the first four generations of communication breakthrough within humanity.

Before 1400's, paper and books were very expensive and rare. Knowledge was passed down generally by word-of mouth. Most languages were generally oral with very few scholarly types who could read. In the 1400's the printing press was invented which made printed communication much less rare. This made the transfer

---

[1]Federal Avaiation Administration website
https://www.faa.gov/air_traffic/by_the_numbers/

of knowledge between people relatively much quicker. This first-generation breakthrough caused literacy to greatly increase across Europe and then this greatly affected the United States.

The printing press meant that newspapers became a primary means of communication of news and other events in the 1800's and early 1900's. By the 1800's major newspapers began circulation across the United States delivering knowledge and current events to the masses. Journalism, a whole field of reporting, grew out of the advent of newspapers. The best newspapers were defined by their attention to detail and excellence in presenting the facts of current events. Most newspaper publications were local, but some rose to national and even international stature-especially some newspapers in major global cities such as London or New York.

In the 1920's the first commercial radio broadcasts began being released. Radio broadcasts allowed information to be broadcasted to large numbers of people- if large numbers of people had receivers, they could receive the same broadcast. Family life and entertainment often revolved around radio broadcasts of music, advertising, and other programs. This advent of radio broadcast in relative "real time" represents a 2nd generation breakthrough in mass-media communication. The power of this medium was shown in 1938 when the radio theatre broadcasted *"War of the Worlds"*- a fictional story of the earth suffering invasion from Mars. The radio theatre was mistaken by many to be breaking news, causing widespread panic followed by outrage.

Around the same time, Cinematography and motion pictures were in their infancy. Movie theatres opened in many cities where people could see a motion picture show with sound. This would cause Hollywood, California to become the center of the film industry. The main problem with motion pictures is that video or motion picture could not be broadcasted in "real time". Films depicting current international events needed to be shipped across the sea after being filmed- this would still take weeks.

Around the same time, telephones became common in the United States. It became possible to talk to other people in other parts of the country through using the telephone-but it was still a device that only wealthier Americans could afford. One of the most famous polling misses in the 1930's was a telephone poll predicting Franklin D. Roosevelt would lose badly. The problem is that the vast majority of U.S. voters at that time did not have a telephone. This changed in the 1940's-1950's and beyond. Cell phones became common beginning in the 1980's.

The third-generation communication breakthrough occurred with advent of public and commercial television broadcasting. The first television broadcasts were in black and white- but color television was just around the corner. Live events could now be broadcasted in "real time" as they were occurring. Some notable events broadcasted live include the bulletin that President Kennedy had been shot in 1963, the beginning of the Persian Gulf War in 1991 during the evening dinner news hour, the space shuttle disaster in 1987, Presidential debates, and numerous notable sporting events. The advent of television and radio helped businesses quickly advertise new goods and services to large numbers of people. The advent of mass-media broadcasting also rapidly transformed politics and political messaging as well.

Along with television came the advent of home video games in the 1980's and then advancements in 1990's. Prior to the 1980's video games were only available in limited amounts of sophistication in arcades. Soon, other gaming systems could be hooked up to a television and allow kids of all ages to play video games in their own home. It was found that messaging in the forms of advertising or subliminal messages could be incorporated into video games. In addition, computer games were becoming more popular as well- much video game technology involved electronic technology that could also apply to building stronger and faster computers.

Computers were to bring a forth generational breakthrough in communication technology along with an impact on commerce likened to the industrial revolution. The internet actually started in the 1950's to link military and university research computer networks together. World-wide protocol was developed in the 1970's enabling computers to send information to one another.

Up until the 1990's working on computers was thought of as more of a "nerd" fringe activity. Computers were big and bulky. It was generally thought that you could only run one computer program on the computer at one time and the emphasis was on building larger computer programs. With advent of Microsoft windows, it made it possible to run several computer programs at once, making computing much faster and easier. Bill Gates and Paul Allen basically transformed global society with this invention.

With the advent of Windows for computers, it became possible to both search the budding internet for information and apply it in another computer program seamlessly. It was possible to connect to the internet via phone systems. Web browsers made searching various topics for information much faster via computer networks. The downloading of knowledge was still somewhat slow- only a kilobytes per second. However, faster internet connections were just around the corner. High speed fiber-optic internet connections made it possible to download information much faster. High-speed internet connections increased from kilobytes to megabytes to gigabytes per second after the turn of the 21st century.

While computing speeds and the ability to download information increased dramatically, the size of computer devices dramatically decreased. Personal desk-top computers became common in households in the 1990's. Laptops became common in the first decade of the 21th century. Mobile phones that are basically computers have become common in the 2010's. Cameras and film production in dark rooms have been replaced by mobile phones that are able to take pictures and video. Digital communication makes it possible to instantly transmit video and pictures to other people through the internet and mobile phone data.

The digital breakthrough and an explosion of knowledge

The digital revolution and the rise of social media represent the fifth generation of breakthrough in mass-broadcasting and communication technology. It is possible to do large-scale broadcasting and communication while also getting instant feedback. Projects, such as translating a language can be worked upon by thousands across the world through group sourcing. Throughout history, total human knowledge doubled roughly every century. This with all these travel and communicational breakthroughs, the time it took human knowledge to double has decreased dramatically. The total amount of knowledge available now doubles virtually every year and the rate of doubling knowledge is exponentially becoming faster.

Much banking and other financial transactions are done on-line. An online presence for stores and other businesses are very important as much marketing, buying, and selling occurs on-line. For example, I could go online and buy stocks from overseas. Large retail centers like Amazon.com are internet-based with the promise of free shipping if you spend enough money at their store or are a premium member. It is possible to pay bills on-line along with transferring money between accounts through the internet. There are some who have attempted to build on-line currencies that transcend national currencies (the dollar, the shekel, pounds etc.) such as bitcoin.

Much entertainment and other activities for pleasure (for example, on-line gaming) occur due to on-line internet connections. For example, it is possible to play a game of chess with virtually anyone across the world. Other online fighting and strategy games are played as well. It is possible to stream movies- and a new generation of graphically generated programs and movies are emerging.

What all this means is that we are connected globally through travel, economics, and communication in ways that were never possible before this generation. Events from half-way around the world can be streamed in "real time" via the internet at the speed of light. For example, someone can watch events occurring in Kansas City from the rice fields in China or Indonesia with only a few seconds delay. We can meet and people from around the world and chat in "real time" through video phones-or we can see people in person from around the world within a day or two through air travel. It is possible for me to consult with a doctor on-line or receive psychological counseling on-line.

Mass-media communication used to be limited to only some people- "important people" such as Presidents, business leaders, and other cultural leaders were the only ones who had access to mass-media. Broadcast stations dictated what would be seen by the masses. However, in the digital age, nearly anyone has access to communicate with the rest of the world. Driven by the communication breakthroughs and the digital revolution, social media platforms such as *Facebook, Twitter, Youtube*, and *Snapchat* have made the news much more personal and instant.

We now have a 24-7 news cycle. As the sun sets in the United States, the sun is rising in Asia. Breaking news from Jerusalem or Tokyo is told around the world. If there is a major disaster like the 2011 Earthquake and Tsunami, we now have live pictures and video in the United States and other nations when such an event would take a few weeks to learn about only a century ago. Economic news spreads through the world at the blink of an eye. Someone can buy stocks in the Shanghai stock exchange from New York City in real time. Multi-million-dollar deals go down quickly in "real time" through internet technology apparently every day.

With the advent and widespread use of personal social media, it is now possible for anyone to report or even make the news with a video shot by phone. Sending a message or a video (through cell phones and laptop computers) that can reach large numbers of people and has a huge impact. How many videos shot by "common people" have gone "viral" on the internet through continuous sharing on social media transforming them from "common people" to "celebrity status" overnight?

Social media platforms and the internet have also made tech giants such *Facebook, Google, Apple, Twitter, Youtube* and other search engines or social media platforms to be extremely important "gatekeepers" of society and culture in the United States. They make the rules and regulations based on what is promoted on their internet platforms and what is not. Since they are private companies, they are not required to conform to the rules of "freedom of speech" guaranteed by the U.S. constitution. Progressive globalists have aggressivelytargeted these media platforms to effectively silence those who have opposing views.

The rapid advancement of travel and human technology are crucial to understanding the end-hope of the gospel of globalism. Only 120 years ago, humanity was still generally traveling with horses and trains; "motor wagons" were rare-and yet look at how far we have come technologically. Humanity does things that only one or two generations ago, people thought were impossible. With the exponential growth of technology and knowledge, what isn't possible in the future for humanity to collectively achieve?

Meanwhile, biblical Christians believe that the rapid exponential increase of knowledge along with the ease of long-distance travel was predicted more than 2,500 years ago by the prophet Daniel (Daniel 12:4) and implied 2,000 years ago by John the Apostle (in the book of Revelation). Could this mean that awesome and terrifying events predicted by Daniel and the Apostle John (and others) could take place in our generation? Many liken the rapid, exponential increase of knowledge as a remake of the tower of Babel- not with brick and tar; but with silicon and electronics. Which narrative is the trusted and important one?

In any case, the advent of computer digital technology has drastically changed society in the 21st century-in how we do things. A whole generation of teenagers and young adults are growing up not remembering when there was no internet available. Along with the physical technology and the way society in the United States does things, the digital revolution has also profoundly affected the culture, influence, and the structure of human relationships in the United States (and worldwide). To this, we must now turn our attention to.

Chapter 6: Today's culture of Offense

Last chapter, we looked at the impact of the technological revolution in travel, communications, and digital speed. Travel is fast, efficient, and much safer than 150 years ago-especially long-distance travel. News that took weeks to deliver 150 years ago can now be delivered within minutes. We are all much more aware of the global picture than we were even 50 years ago. The digital revolution, the rise of social media, and the heightened speed of travel have deeply affected how we do things in this generation. It also affects how this generation thinks about itself-and sets up a generation to receive a secular narrative known as "The Gospel of Globalism".

<u>The "know-it-all generation"</u>

Education of teenagers and young adults has drastically changed with the internet access to information. Fifty years ago, if youth or young adults didn't know something, they would ask an older adult to get the knowledge and understanding. In the digital age, anyone can simply look up the information or a video on "how to" via their phone or computer on the internet. Why wait for information from inquiring of an older generation when you can get instant information via the internet?

Who can afford to wait to get the information with a fast-paced society like today- in order to make important snap decisions? How can we tell if an older generation is not simply using the flow of information to influence our behavior? This is the generation where questioning everything is considered okay unlike generations past. This societal change has it roots in the field of physical science.

Sir Isaac Newton's discoveries in the areas of mathematics and physics helped build the modern world including the industrial revolution. According to Sir Isaac Newton discoveries in physics and mathematics, the natural world was rather predictable. Modern thought focused on predictability stability of structures, and immovability.

However, things changed with Einstein's theory of relativity along with the open display of power through splitting of the atom (or fusing them together). Newton's laws of physics still generally worked-relative to the energy and speed of light (E=mc2)- as everything is relatively close to "0" compared to the speed of light. However, when particles approached the speed of light, these "tried, tested, and true" laws of Newtonian physics began to warp.

The explosive open demonstration of Einstein's theories of relativity sent shockwaves across the earth in understanding science, governmental institutions, and even morality. Instead of simply assuming everything taught was true it was now right to question everything. Anything found to be inconsistent could and should have been torn down. Our understanding of philosophy and knowledge began to change.

In a generation with huge amounts of knowledge at its fingertips, how could a "pecking order" be established in society to bring cultural order? In previous generations, the amount of intelligence was key- measured by intelligence quotient (IQ) along with physical attributes such as strength and stamina. Relational skill was important, but under-recognized. However, with all the information we could ever want, this has changed rather dramatically in a generation.

A key differentiator among today's youth and young adults is emotional intelligence quotient (EQ) instead of intelligence quotient (IQ). With easy access to plenty of information, the key issue among our culture becomes, "who can strategically out-maneuver other people situationally and relationally" to gain a decisive advantage? Among a younger generation, games such as *Settlers of Catan*, *Dominion*, and Poker are quite popular-and they all have this motif in their game play. On-line games such as *Doom* and other war games pit teams of players with various abilities up against other teams in virtual combat. Popular broadcast shows such as *Survivor* and *Big Brother* reinforce this motif. Theoretically with all the information at our disposal, it should automatically mean that we can make good decisions.

The convenience of the world of common knowledge at our fingertips has come with hidden, but very steep price. First, the unending flow of information and 24-7 news cycle has created a restless generation dependent on coffee, energy bars, and energy drinks. The danger of sleeping for a young generation is that someone could miss an earth-shattering event and suddenly find themselves irrelevant culturally or economically. This has served to connect us more with our phones and information and less with each other. The resulting lack of sleep and increased stress leads to a higher risk of getting offended if things do not go "the right way".

Second, there is unfortunately also a great difference between knowledge and wisdom. While knowledge can be acquired almost instantly in the digital generation, acquiring wisdom does not work this way: Wisdom is acquired by experience (and survival)- something the older generations have which a younger generation will inherently not have.

For example, the wisdom of saving some money is clearly not a top priority among youth as they may miss-out on a great opportunity NOW. However, many are saying that this younger generation is likely to have less than older generations- why? In general, wealth is built up incrementally over time based on compound interest. A whole generation is finding this out at the hands of credit-card lenders who charge huge amounts of interest on customers to use their credit cards. This same principle applies to many other pursuits that are important such as business, raising a family, and simply doing life. Unfortunately, youth is often accompanied by stupidity and vulnerability. Young people can easily be taken advantage of- by shrewd, manipulative older people and systems.

In past generations, in the midst of inquiring of older adults, relationship bonding took place and trust was built. More than knowledge, wisdom was passed down from generation to generation through trust. It is very true that an older generation is generally less "in touch" with the latest digital and technological trends. However, an older generation is much more "in touch" with human nature, dealing with people, and how to spot when people are lying or manipulating. However, with the explosion of digital access to all the information anyone could ever want, this generation has become a "know-it-all" culture among the youth-who don't need a generation of fathers. All this has helped create real gaps between the generations.

Generational brokenness:

This generation is also perhaps the most emotionally broken generation in history as well. The statistics are rather staggering: Roughly 1 in 2 marriages end in divorce. Seeing the difficulty and heartache associated with marriage, there are also large numbers of people who cohabitate with each other (including sex) without ever getting married. The "traditional" core family of mother, father, and children is now the exception rather than the norm. Large numbers of children grow up in single parent or "blended" families with step-mothers or step-fathers. Recently in 2014, the U.S. government sanctioned homosexual marriages as legal, creating situations where children could have two mothers or two fathers. The education system is attempting to pass off this family structure as normal- yet why doesn't this occur regularly in the animal kingdom? The changing of understanding of "normal" family structure is fertile ground for the gospel of globalism to spring forth. How did we get to this point in the United States of America? We need to take a look back at the last few generations.

Many of the generation that endured the great depression and fought WWII saw things that were absolutely horrific: death, disease, destruction, and despair. In order to endure such difficult situations, many men stuffed these horrible emotions. Unfortunately, this also caused serious relational bonding problems in fathering the next generation. This led to an emotionally "frozen" generation" of men that fathered a generation of children known as "The Baby Boomers"- who came of age in the late 1950's and especially the 1960's.

As the 1960's started, a young adult generation known as the "baby boomer" generation was becoming quite distrustful of American institutions. Several high-profile scandals involving healing evangelists along with a growing sense of hypocrisy within the church caused a generation to begin questioning the motives of the institutional Church. New scientific theories on the origins of life (that we'll look at next chapter) began to emerge- causing a generation to question the societal authority of Church teachings on things such as morality, origins of life, and faith in general.

The assassination of John F. Kennedy and the Vietnam War shook a generation's trust in government: Was the U.S. government truly benevolent or was there something sinister happening? There was tension with the Soviet Union and communism. Meanwhile, nuclear weapons presented a frightening possibility that this generation could be the last generation if another world war broke out. In addition, television brought troubling images of civil rights protesters and the white majority's violent response across the south as the structural racism hidden but resident in the culture was now on full display.

Add all these factors to a lack of wisdom by young adults-and it is really no surprise that there was widespread rebellion. The 1967 "Summer of Love" in San Francisco along with "Woodstock" in 1969 released a powerful sexual revolution in America. Before then, pre-marital sex was strongly looked down upon and carried a stigma.

After these two events, the stigma of pre-marital sex began lifting off the culture.

While the stigma of pre-marital sex began lifting off American culture, the impacts of this revolution on families and relationships continued to unfold. Sex and marriage were no longer considered automatically sacred (though still valued) among the boomers and the divorce rate gradually began to increase. Abortion was legalized in 1973-apparently creating a quick and easy "fix" to the problem of pregnancy caused by sex outside the covenant of marriage. Since 1973, roughly 60 million people have been aborted in their mother's womb.

In the midst of all these cultural changes, large segments of Church were preaching messages warning of the wrath of God coming along with utter destruction. Yet, all these sinful, rebellion against scripture things happened in the 1960's and 1970's without any overt, large-scale open displays of what could openly and easily be perceived as "the judgment of God" in global natural disasters or world wars. A whole generation coming out of the baby-boomers in the 1970's and 1980's was "me-centered"-as children of a relationally broken generation. Divorce rates skyrocketed. The percentage of people attending church weekly dropped drastically. Biblical literacy plummeted as a "progressive understanding of Christianity" began to take root in the culture.

Some historians have called this generation, "Generation X" because the lack of a massive event that this generation could identify with such as World War II, (The GI generation) or the Post-World War II economic boom and celebration (baby-boomers). Other historians might call this generation the "baby buster" generation due to the legalization of abortion. Still others could call this generation the "me" generation.

The generation born in the 1970's and the 1980's has now given birth to a new generation of youth and young adults. This generation has many of the same characteristics of the "me generation" except, they have grown up with in the era of internet, social media, and 24-7. This current generation has also been deeply marked by the events of September 11ᵗʰ, 2001 where Islamic jihadists flew planes into the World Trade Center in New York City and at targets in Washington DC killing almost 3,000 people. The result was a world-wide "war on terror" involving military action in Afghanistan and Iraq but this "war on terror" goes far deeper than military action.

A deeper issue that many have been looking at beginning in the 1990's is, "what is the root cause of the problem"? There has been more of an emphasis on this related to criminal rehabilitation and other deviant behavior within cultures and society as a whole. This has also given rise to programs aimed at preventing deviant behavior in general- addressing the "root causes" of terrorism. The agricultural theory is that if you take out the visible problem (the plant) above ground, it won't eliminate the problem. Instead, if the roots are taken out, the whole system causing the problem will disappear. One of the targets of this generation's "war on terror": intolerant religion (jihadism in Islam), but the same danger could also exist in other religions. This has given rise to an emphasis on finding the deep root issues that cause problems.

A culture where offense is normative:

A big "root" problem that even global humanists have found is offense leading to bitterness. No one likes to be bitter because bitterness hurts emotionally and physically. Even several secular medical studies have confirmed that holding grudges and bitterness is really bad for long-term physical health; weakening the immune system, and increasing the risk of heart disease, strokes, and cancer.

The epidemic of offended people is spilling over into public violence- including mass-shootings that terrorize the public. Mass-shootings used to get instant headline news in the 1990's or 2000's.

As of 2019, they no longer get the main headlines unless dozens are killed. We train for public "active shooter" incidents as if they are like fire drills; something unheard of in the 1990's. This has helped perpetuate a culture of fear of offending people; and a culture of offense. The next question is: How do we deal with severe offense and preventing offense?

First, according to humanism and globalism, some offenses are so severe emotionally that they are impossible to recover from. From a secular humanistic point of view, forgiveness is simply relative for our own sakes. The only thing that can satisfy and fix the offense is the unleashing of justice where the offenders are punished and reparations are fully made-including damages from emotional suffering. Whole social justice movements to "fix" deep- rooted offenses in culture have risen up. For example, the movement to legalize homosexual marriage and make it normative in the culture has risen up in response to how practicing homosexuals have been deeply hurt and offended by the Christian majority.

Second, the threat of offense has given rise to a culture of "tolerance"- do everything you possibly can to avoid offending people. The misuse of power economically and socially is a particularly sensitive spot. Since Christianity and an apparent "Christian worldview" has dominated American culture, secular humanists have emphasized Christians practicing tolerance towards other worldviews by not speaking out against them based on what the Bible says in order to avoid offending people. Saying or doing something against this cultural doctrine of tolerance is very offensive and not to be tolerated.

As more secularists are awaking to the potential that they are now the pluralistic majority, this is leading to a much more complicated scenario-what now? Ironically, the level of offense is even greater today than it was in the 1980's and 1990's. Instead of forbearance and even overlooking offense; things that cause offense cannot be overlooked by a "know it all" generation. Anything that offends is taken as a direct attack against their identity as part of the "know it all" generation.

The 2016 election put this deep divide on full display as well as the 2018 election. Due to a culture of offense, it is nearly impossible to carry on a political or religious discussion (where there is significant disagreement) without someone exploding in anger. Those who adhere to the Gospel of Globalism narrative say part of the problem is the lack of information or knowledge and that more applied knowledge is to critical to understanding what causes offense and avoiding offense.

Meanwhile, this viewpoint contradicts the biblical warning that an increase in knowledge itself can lead to dangerous amounts of arrogant pride without dependence upon God in Deuteronomy 8, 32, and Romans 1:18-32. According to the Bible, arrogant pride often manifests in offense and bitterness. To those who have been hurt and forgiven, they have found that it take humility actually forgive others. Yet, the Bible claims, it is impossible to remove the problem of offense through any other way. King Solomon had virtually everything- incredible knowledge, wisdom, honor, wealth, the operation of the supernatural, authority and rulership over a prosperous kingdom, a harem of women, and peace with neighboring nations. Yet, his life ended with great bitterness to the point where he sought to kill a threat to his throne much like King Saul. The Bible flat-out warns that knowledge puffs up leading to pride and rebellion which leads to "bitter fruit".

Offense and bitterness is painful physically, emotionally, and mentally. Offense is rampant in today's culture- and makes a generation vulnerable. Often, people are willing to do whatever it takes to remove a short-term source of bitterness or pain -even if it is detrimental in the long-term. What is the solution? The Bible says that offense and bitterness is the result of conceit and arrogance-and that the only solution is to humble ourselves and forgive; even if what others did was apparently "unforgivable". Multiple scriptures clearly warn Christians that they MUST forgive in order to be forgiven by Jesus.

However, humanistic globalism sort of offers another solution: We don't have the solution yet-so need to practice tolerance and grow in knowledge until we get the perfect knowledge and understanding of each other to avoid getting offended. While we don't understand the roots of the problem of offense in the culture, we suspect it is dogmatic religion with moral absolutes. Why come to this conclusion?

Over the next three chapters, we next need to look at some basic arguments for the Gospel of Globalism narrative: Where did we come from? What about spirituality and globalism (who are we)? Is there a great globalism future hope? It is into this cultural context that, "the gospel of globalism" is presented over the next three chapters-and a little bit on how it contrasts to the biblical gospel narrative. This is predictive based on technology and understanding not quite developed yet but is in the heart of scientists and researchers worldwide. The Gospel of Globalism narrative in our culture today addresses deep longings in the human heart and will affect our future. However, was this contemporary Gospel of Globalism narrative previously predicted in generations past?

Chapter 7: The Gospel of Globalism narrative- where did we come from?

Fundamental to understanding a gospel narrative are the questions of identity for each member of humanity: Where did I come from? Who am I? Where is this going? The Bible gives clear understanding to these questions: God created everything seen and unseen as Creator. The complexity of life on the earth (from an atomic level) is testimony to the incredible knowledge, wisdom, and brilliance of God. We are created by God in the image of God (Genesis 1-2; Psalm 139 etc.). We are deeply beloved by God (John 3:16 etc.). We were meant to dwell with God forever (Revelation 21-22). The Biblical gospel also gives each of us a choice to honor God's definitions of right and wrong and then do things God's way through Jesus Christ leading to everlasting life or do it our own way, leading to everlasting destruction.

Charles Darwin on natural selection and survival of the Fittest.

However, there is a powerful alternative narrative strung together by humanist globalists that also answers these three questions. First, we need to look at the origins of humanity: Where did we come from? According to the secular humanist globalism narrative, we are all incredibly lucky. At the moment of conception, there were millions of male sperm attempting to get to "the one female egg" (or two for twins, three for triplets etc.). We are the production of the "one" that made it.

I am describing what biology calls "natural selection" or "survival of the fittest". First observed by Charles Darwin in the Galapagos islands over time, he observed that some physical characteristics within a species of animals were more desirable than others. As the result those who had desirable physical characteristics would eventually become more numerous while those with not desirable physical characteristics would diminish in population and eventually die off and become extinct. He published his observations over time in the landmark scientific paper, *The Origins of Species.*

We can see the same things occurring within human economics- in the struggle to survive (financially), those who have the best technology and advantageous characteristics within their products will defeat those who have lesser technology and advantageous characteristics within their products such as cameras, cars, etc. A capitalist economy thrusts human innovation and technology forward simply to survive and prosper economically- it is survival of the fittest and natural selection within each industry.

Where things get more complicated is when we begin talking about whole industry fields...does one industrial field supersede and replace another one? The answer is YES! For example, cassette tapes and tape players used to be THE thing to have in the 1980's- especially a "Walkman"; a small portable radio that played tapes. This has been replaced by CD's and now smart phones that can store thousands of songs. The cassette tape industry is basically gone. The same things have happened related to horses being replaced by cars as THE mode of transportation. The same thing with has happened with military weapons: tanks have replaced chariots as the preferred ground unit. Guns and bombs have replaced swords and shields as the preferred weapons of choice for militaries around the world.

The question then becomes, could biological life forms do the same thing as economic industries do-evolve between species; where one species is superseded and/or replaced by another species? The answer according to the Gospel of Globalism is a presumed yes. It is presumed based on Darwin's observations of natural selection and the famous Stanley Miller experiment of 1952 that biologically, life as we know it spontaneously began with energy, molecules, and water coming together "just right". After all, the universe is a vast beyond measure with galaxies found billions of light-years away. Could life spontaneously initiate somewhere else, given the exact combination of chemistry and astrophysics?

It's sort of like "rolling the dice" related to conditions of necessary to initiate and sustain life according to the globalists. You need a large number of dice (let's say a trillion) to roll "just right" in an exact sequence combination that starts life. (Similar to DNA). Simply rolling all the dice one time and the odds are extremely low-virtually zero. However, if you get to roll the trillion dice an absolutely large number of times like let's say 5 quadrillion, septillion times, the odds start to improve according to the globalist theory on the origination of life. Could the exact correct combination come up more than once? Is there more than one "winning combination" to initiate biological life? Humanistic globalists would answer yes to these critical existential questions. However, they are not promoted openly yet due to the lack of empirical proof of life outside planet earth (yet).

Then narrative continues, over billions of years through natural selection, and "survival of the fittest" life forms eventually evolved into more advanced life-forms (with greater advantages) until humans evolved from other primates. The idea that we are somehow created is very difficult to stomach by globalists- it would imply that if we were created by some higher "being", we are subject to it.

Without getting into all the empirical numbers and odds of all this happening, actual estimates of the odds of life spontaneously beginning differ greatly based on other convictions and worldview. However, it is clear nobody alive today was present to witness the initiation of biological life. In other words, the belief in spontaneous initiation of life by chance (at the foundation of the humanist, globalist narrative) must be taken by faith (based upon limited present evidence); just as much as the belief the biblical accounts of creation is also based upon faith. So, what are the important implications of spontaneous initiation of life, natural selection, and biological evolution?

Implications of evolution and natural selection in the globalism narrative.

According to the Gospel of Globalism, we are incredibly "lucky" to have been the recipients of spontaneous initiation of life on this planet we call earth. It is also easily observable that we must at least maintain the current (extraordinary rare) living environment while looking for more understanding of the "combination" that initiated and sustains life. This has huge implications on how we steward the resources of planet earth.

As the winners in the process of natural selection, survival of the fittest, and evolutionary the highest evolved life form, it means that humans are all extraordinary and special. However, it also means that some are "more special than others" according to the globalism narrative. What differentiates those who are more special than others?

Margaret Sanger, the founding director of planned parenthood believed in natural selection and survival of the fittest. She was very concerned with how humanity was breeding with each other; in how favorable traits of humans to advance evolution were in-breeding with other unfavorable traits. She had the assumption that the white, Anglo-Saxon genetic traits were superior to African-American genetic traits. Margaret Sanger wrote:

It {Eugenics} sees that the most responsible and most intelligent members of society are the less fertile; that the feeble-minded are the more fertile. Herein lies the unbalance, the great biological menace to the future of civilization. Are we heading to biological destruction, toward the gradual but certain attack upon the stocks of intelligence and racial health by the sinister forces of irresponsibility and imbecility? This is not such a remote danger as the optimistic Eugenist might suppose. The mating of a moron with a person of sound stock may, as Dr. Tredgold points out, gradually disseminate this trait far and wide until it undermines the vigor and efficiency of an entire nation and an entire race. This is no idle fancy[2]

While most humanistic globalists condemn Margaret Sanger's overt racism against African Americans and other minority ethnic groups, she is highly regarded by those holding to the globalism narrative.

To globalists, her work implies that some are born with natural traits that are favorable- physical strength, emotional intelligence, strong mental intelligence, and stamina while others are not. Based on "survival of the fittest" and natural selection, it is desirable to eliminate those with traits that are not favorable. Since the forward advancement of the overall human race is desired for the globalists, it means this would imply that some people are "expendable" while other people are not. The value of human beings in this case would be relative: What you do (or can do) determines who you are (on the pecking order of society) and how valuable you really are according to the globalist narrative. All this has huge implications in dealing with issues such as dealing with global over-population, the danger of depleting resources, and environmentalism. Morality becomes relative based on what we as the winners of this universal evolutionary contest decide.

Meanwhile this is in sharp contrast to the biblical narrative and its implications. If God indeed created us in his image it means that all human life is sacred- including those with physical defects, or mental disorders such as schizophrenia, autism, or Down Syndrome. Intentionally murdering someone over a grudge or other typical motives is more than an attack on that person, it is an attack against God himself. People are made in God's image and murder (destroying God's image) must be dealt with in the most severe form (death penalty) to protect the sanctity of human life (Genesis 9:5-7).

---

[2] Maragret Sanger, "The Pivot of Civilization" 1992 Brentanos, p175-176
http://www.zombietime.com/zomblog/?p=1953

<u>In the Globalism narrative, truth is relative (sort of) and morality relative.</u>

Of course, the Bible is full of absolute truth claims. Jesus said, "I am the way, the truth, and the Life…" (John 14:6). The Bible claims that God has absolute authority as creator and sustainer of life to declare what is right and wrong. God thundered the 10 commandments in Exodus 20 for everyone to hear-that are applicable in all cultures, all settings, and all situations. In contrast, the globalist narrative claims that morality is relative between good and evil- based on human experience, and collectively what is for the good of people.

What makes it difficult to maintain moral relativism is that the claim "all truth is relative" is self-contradictory. By saying "all" truth is relative, you are making an absolute truth claim! A better statement for relative moral relativism is that there *could* be absolute truth out there; but there is no way to empirically prove moral truth claims are true at this time. In addition, anyone who claims to have access to absolute truth must be (at this time), "absolutely" wrong according to moral relativists and those who hold to the humanist, globalist narrative. Where is your proof?

Will there ever be a time where morality becomes absolute? Perhaps, but according to globalists, the lack of information and knowledge along with "no empirical proof" of absolute truth in this day and age make absolute truth claims and moral claims very shaky at best; arrogant at worst.

With the lack of credible absolute truth claims, what are globalists left with in terms of determining morality; right and wrong? This is where things get complicated. While there may not be "moral absolutes" according to globalists, there is a lot of empirical, observational evidence in that doing some things are very harmful to personal health and other things are beneficial to individual personal health. For example, holding grudges is bad for physical health while eating healthy and regular exercise is generally good for physical health and well-being. Thus what is "good" is what benefits us and what is "bad" is what harms us individually.

The same empirical evidence also applies to society at large. There is a lot of evidence that certain behaviors are good and that other behaviors are bad for societal health. There must be a balance between natural selection, "survival of the fittest", and overall progress for the species (greatest common good). These two pillars are the foundations for globalist morality.

If it were simply natural selection and "survival of the fittest"- morality would be non-existent. Everyone would simply do what is right in their own eyes. This would lead to situations that would be good for individuals temporarily but bad for humanity in general. For example, looting a storehouse during a famine disaster (where there is little food as the result for society) would be good for the individual doing the looting, but really bad for everyone else. In terms of a moral relativity- it would be impossible to challenge: who is to say that you are right and I am wrong?

Even humanists can observe that there are symbiotic relationships between species in biology- where relationship with cooperation is beneficial for both species involved. This is the theory behind the assembly line, mass-production, and the division of labor. Rather than have everyone do everything (when some people are gifted at doing some things, while not gifted at doing other things). Why not have everyone do what they are gifted at in the right places? Then collectively we can accomplish more together. This is particularly true if there is no- infighting within the collective team for favored roles and where the human dynamics encourage everyone involved on the team to excel.

This is the theory behind symbiotic relationships and collective morality: some regular behaviors (such as rude behavior, intolerant behavior, sexism, bullying etc.) are bad for collective whole and need to be condemned and punished in our communities. Other behaviors such as self-sacrifice or hard work for the good of the whole are considered virtuous. Everything becomes relative as the interaction between human beings (especially cross-culturally) becomes extremely complicated. However, technology is beginning to bridge these cultural and even linguistic gaps with language programs such as "google translate".

Of course, there are behaviors that are so destructive to society (such as murder, rape, treason, leading oppressive regimes that produce genocide etc.) that they must be punished-but how? Globalist humanists are divided on the issue- some believe that administering the death penalty is making an absolute claim that their behavior is morally wrong contradicting relativism- but something must be done to neutralize their behavior and make a public statement that such behavior is not helpful to the collective species. Thus, there is a push to end the death penalty in favor of life in prison without parole and if necessary, completely isolate them from the rest of society including the rest of the prison population. Perhaps, the inherit goodness of humanity will come out through total isolation.

Of course, according to the globalist narrative, even killing off certain people may even be justifiable in order to stop their on-going menace to society (greatest common good). There are people who are simply "monsters". Also, there is clearly a problem of suffering and pain within humanity. One of the key issues globalists face is the issue of spirituality and religion: Who exactly are we (as humanity)? In understanding the Gospel of Globalism next, we must look at the questions of spirituality and religion.

Chapter 8:   The Gospel of Globalism– the problem of religion and suffering.

The issue of religion and spirituality presents perhaps the greatest challenge to Gospel of Globalism narrative. Large numbers of people have shared their testimonies of supernatural healings that have been confirmed by medical professionals. An increasing number of people have also testified of supernatural visions of the afterlife publicly on shows such as the *It's supernatural with Sid Roth*. The empirical evidence of "something else out there" is growing. There are a growing number of unexplained, "supernatural" events people have testified to-some even verified by doctors. There is an increasing number of videos where the "supernatural" was documented on camera. This has great implications for who we are individually and as a human race, our understanding of right from wrong, tackling the problem of human suffering, explaining where we came from, and where this is going.

Is there a way to explain this? Judaism and Biblical Christianity has quite an easy explanation: The Bible clearly records the activities of angelic beings in the gospels, Acts, and elsewhere, like the book of Daniel and Revelation. The Bible also infers angelic activity all throughout the scriptures. They are (normally) invisible spirits that influence life today for the sake of God's purposes in individuals, families, cities, and nations. Meanwhile, the scripture also refers to a satanic kingdom of fallen angels that is also at work against individuals, families, cities, and nations in conflict with angelic activity (Revelation 12).

The Bible is also full of supernatural activity in both the Hebrew Scriptures and the New Testament. Numerous miracles are recorded in the book of Genesis and Exodus-some downright terrifying. The gospels record that Jesus Christ healed the sick, cast out demons, performed other miracles and raised the dead. Jesus then commanded his disciples to do likewise (Matthew 10:8; 28:18-20; Mark 16:15-20). The book of Acts records the apostles doing likewise in obedience to Jesus. There is sporadic documentation of supernatural events throughout history-but they are few and far between. Then suddenly in the 20th and the 21st century, there has been an explosion of these "supernatural reports".

Apparently random spirituality and the globalist narrative.

Adherents to the Gospel of Globalism argue that miracles and supernatural phenomena are not simply associated with Judaism and Christianity. Some other religions don't overtly teach on the supernatural but there are clearly groups in them that attempt to reach the supernatural realm. Islam began with a reported visitation of an angel to Mohammed and other supernatural events surrounding the writing of the Quran. The founder of Buddhism had an "enlightening experience" (perhaps supernatural) as well. Mormonism began with some sort of supernatural visitation to Joseph Smith. There are other esoteric practices out there as well such as Freemasonry, Vo-doo, divination, necromancy, and casting spells that the Bible condemns. There are reports of statues of Mary bleeding and apparent appearances of the Virgin Mary. There are apparently some anecdotes of other "supernatural events" happening in these other religions as well. What in heaven or earth is happening?

As the result of these reports, religious pilgrimages occur from most spiritual backgrounds. Roman Catholics pilgrimage to sites where the Virgin Mary reportedly appeared. Meanwhile, Hindus also do pilgrimages and spend large amounts of money in order to reincarnate into a better life with the hopes of reaching Nirvana. Buddhists pilgrimage to high places to meditate and practice the 8-fold path with the desire to be free of all desires. Meanwhile Muslims are commanded to make their once-in-a- lifetime pilgrimage to Mecca. Jews pilgrimage to Jerusalem (if they can) to celebrate the high holy days including Passover.

All these reports of "supernatural experiences" are beginning to make it clear that an anti-supernatural, atheistic worldview may need to evolve-where better theories supersede other theories. Something is out there we don't fully understand yet. Aliens? UFO's?

A simple atheistic, humanistic worldview is becoming problematic to hold as new scientific theories are beginning to spring forth. This would imply the need of scientific theories to evolve around these "supernatural events" as well. According to globalists, perhaps the next advancement in human evolution is at hand, but the evolution may be "spiritual" involving the exponential increase in knowledge and harnessing what we now call "the supernatural"-according to the Gospel of Globalism narrative.

The Gospel of Globalism narrative begins its case by stating how the supernatural seems so unpredictable. Why does the operation of the supernatural look to be so random and still relatively rare? It appears on the surface that supernatural occurrences are random. Many agnostics became such because they asked God to do something that would have really helped them "get ahead" of other people or heal a dying relative- only for the answer to be a disappointing "no answer" that causes deep pain and offense. We know from empirical studies that holding bitterness and is bad for physical health so the easy way to deal with this problem is to conclude that the "supernatural realm" operates in an apparent random fashion-or does it?

To bolster the first part of the case the globalism narrative would cite examples of healing evangelists (even back in the 1950's) who perhaps operated in some sort of supernatural healing "gift"-but some of them fell into public sin scandals (according to Bible-thumping fundamentalist Christians). Added evidence are the cases of failed "prophetic predictions" that fundamentalist Christians have released- that of course, have not come true. Finally, another source of apparent randomness and adding to the confusion is that some Christians do not preach against sin but only emphasize God's benevolence- and people still experience supernatural healing or comfort through them. How do these things actually work? Are these supernatural "powers" dangerous? Can a "supernatural power" be understood and "tamed" to operate on-demand based on the needs or desires of people? There are many unanswered questions about religion, spirituality, and possible "hidden" sources of power.

Human nature, sin, and the problem of human suffering...

The Bible clearly touches on human nature- Beginning in Genesis 3, man disobeyed God after being tempted by a serpent to eat from the Tree of the Knowledge of Good and Evil. Following the disobedience of man, the rest of the Bible describes in often graphic detail, the deeds of people that are condemned as wicked and evil. Cain killed Abel. Lamech killed someone and then justified his actions to other people- someone had offended him or hurt him in some way! The men of Sodom surrounded Lot's house and demanded that Lot allow them come and molest the visiting messengers. The Bible warns that the heart of man is deceitful and desperately wicked. The Bible declares that all have sinned and fallen short of God's glory (Romans 3:23). The Bible then says that sin ends in death- physical death and eternal separation from God (the exact opposite of what God intended) in a place of torment that Jesus often warned of. A deeper study of the sin in the Bible indicates that sin acts like cancer: It grows and spreads bringing destruction, pain, and death to everything-unless decisively dealt with.

Sin is the ultimate source of human suffering and pain, but according to the Bible, God has not yet chosen to rid the earth of the presence of sin and the experience of suffering. However, at the core of the Biblical gospel message, Jesus died on a cross in the an excruciating way to bear the full anger of God, openly display how God feels about sin, and make a way for humanity to be reconciled to the one, Trinitarian God through Jesus: fully God and fully man. The Bible then records Jesus rose from the dead as a sign and wonder that the substitutionary sacrifice had been accepted by God.

It is also a sign that God can redeem the deepest brokenness, pain, and suffering and make something beautiful out of it.

Meanwhile, the depravity of humanity is in sharp contrast to the Gospel of Globalism narrative of the nature of humanity: The gospel of globalism declares that humanity is intrinsically good-citing children as evidence: Yes they are inherently selfish-evidence of natural selection, evolution, and "survival of the fittest". However, as children grow up, they also supposedly grow in empathy, understanding, and sophistication-evidence that they understand the notion of "greater common good" for the rest of humanity. While according to the Gospel of Globalism human nature is good, what then are the sources of the experience of human pain, sorrow, and suffering?

Those who adhere to the Gospel of Globalism would cite two massive sources of pain and suffering in the human experience: the lack of knowledge and understanding along with dogmatic, stubborn unwillingness to change- when confronted with superior knowledge and understanding- especially stubborn religious beliefs. Both lead to suffering and offense. Growing individual and corporate knowledge is typically always looked at as a good thing: Knowledge is power! As previously described, the ability to apply knowledge in action is a very desirable trait to the human race. Properly applied knowledge can both give understanding of why someone did something to hurt us and give understanding to practice tolerance and avoid hurting someone else in human relational situations. Applied knowledge can also possibly predict if someone or a group of people present a real danger to life or well-being. What if the ability to rapidly apply knowledge was unleashed to the extreme?

Applied knowledge can also prevent or minimize pain, suffering, and loss from natural causes such as tornadoes, hurricanes, droughts, earthquakes etc. However, this is where the lack of knowledge becomes utterly apparent: We can somewhat predict these natural disasters (minimizing pain, loss, and even death), but how do we *stop* or *prevent* these disasters? Is it possible to cheat death and the terrifying unknown after death (if it is bad)? This is where humanity's lack of knowledge comes into play. However, even with limited knowledge, adherents of the Gospel of Globalim narrative can clearly draw the conclusion that stubborn dogmatic religious belief is THE problem.

The chief problem of humanity: oppressive religion?

Globalists will cite religion (especially mono-theistic religions) as the source of most of the destructive wars and cultural oppression of history. Ever since Northern Israel was wiped out by Assyria, and Judah and southern Israel was wiped out by Babylon, both groups generally held out to the bitter end, resulting in untold suffering. The same thing happened again around AD 70 when the Roman empire once again burned Jerusalem to the ground.

Historically, religion (especially state-sponsored religion) has been used to help maintain order in society-and oppress people. Hinduism has been used to strengthen the Caste system in India causing the oppression of millions. Shintoism and Emperor Worship helped to emphasize loyalty to the state in Japan. There are of course examples of this in western civilization such as Italy being affiliated with Roman Catholicism and of course the Jews with the affiliation with Judaism. However, Gospel of Globalism adherents believe dogmatic religion is the chief reason why human beings are stubborn and will not change-causing much conflict and pain.

Organized religion has also helped fuel wars- "our side" is absolutely right while "the other side" is absolutely wrong. There were the Muslim conquests beginning in the 600's across leading to wars in the Middle East and then into Europe. There were the crusades- the Catholic Church justified slaughtering Muslims to take back the Middle East (particularly Jerusalem). Then there were the huge number of wars fought within Europe between Protestants who had reportedly discovered a new understanding of Biblical

Christianity with the Catholics and their long history and tradition. Sometimes, there were wars between Protestant groups as well. Even if not a direct cause, religion was an underlying worldview factor in fueling World War I; World War II, the Korean War, Vietnam, the Cold War, and the Persian Gulf war (really a slaughter of Iraq's military more than a real war). Dogmatic religion is behind the ongoing wars in Nigeria, fueling ISIS, and the Israeli-Palestinian conflict.

There are the obviously destructive cults led by Jim Jones, David Koresh, and a host of other lesser-known ones that became radicalized mutants. The poor, unsuspecting members were blindly led to their doom by crazed cultic leaders. There are the cult-followings of many who preach promises of health and wealth to the poor in order secure their financial loyalty-while almost completely failing to deliver on their promises. Meanwhile, Christianity and other religions are behind the colonization and oppression of cultures such as Haiti, and many nations in Africa (through slavery). While organized religion belief sometimes brings out the best in humanity, generally it has brought out the worst according to the Gospel of Globalism. According to the globalism narrative, all organized religion is generally a bad thing: especially the dogmatic mono-theistic religions.

The Gospel of Globalism narrative is surprisingly compatible with most theological belief systems such as Hinduism, Buddhism, and pretty much every other esoteric, non-monotheism practice. Hinduism focuses on Karma (what goes around comes around...) with the hopes of eventually achieving the ecstasy of nirvana. Buddhism tends to focus on meditation and tolerance with the hopes of eventually achieving freedom from desires (that lead to suffering) or the beauty of being free of desire. Other more esoteric religions point to "something out there" but we don't have the knowledge of what it is yet. Yet these other religions are generally poly-theistic in their viewpoints. They generally focus on wisdom (applying knowledge) and tolerance of others- something the Gospel of Globalism favors.

The globalist narrative and Islam

Islam presents an interesting challenge and potential opportunity for the globalism narrative. Muslims respect the Jewish prophets and Jesus- but they believe that Mohammed was the prophet that supersedes them all. At first glance they appear to contradict the globalist humanistic narrative and are a great threat to the globalism ambitions- especially in how Islam is currently practiced.

The pictures and video of ISIS beheading infidels is very chilling. Ji-hadist, Islamic Fundamentalism is the theology that drove the hi-jackers to alter the political-religious axis on September 11th, 2001 along with a myriad of other lesser known but still very destructive terroristic attacks. The way Muslims practice their religion currently is very oppressive to women-yet it garners great devotion from its followers that is generally not present in Christianity or Judaism. Due to the devotion of its followers, Islam deeply permeates the whole culture of nations when it is the dominant religion. This would appear to be huge threat to the Gospel of Globalism narrative.

However, a deeper look at Islamic theology would suggest otherwise- due to two main issues: abrogation and the life of Mohammed combined with Islamic eschatology. First with the term "abrogation" is the equivalent of "replacement theology" suggesting evolution is possible. The Quran itself claims that older verses are superseded by newer verses[3]. Islam honors the Jewish prophets and Jesus (Christianity) as prophets. However, Islam believes that Mohammed superseded them all to be God's messenger-but Mohammed never claimed to be God in the flesh. The core of Islam

---

[3] Quran- Sura 2:106; Sura 16:101

appears to be built on theological evolution of Mohammed- something at the core of the Gospel of Globalism narrative.

The life of Mohammed was very unique and interesting. As a merchant, he was able to unite warring merchants in the city of Mecca who worshipped multiple gods into worshipping Allah. As the result he was able to unite them into a fighting force under one religion and set of religious tenants. They nearly conquered the world for Islam. Meanwhile Mohammed believed in the Mahdi who would later come and do what he did-and then some- to prepare the earth for the end. Islam also included a very powerful adversary at the very end that must be conquered.

Within Islam are the seeds of evolution- just like the typical globalism narrative indicates must happen. Obviously, there are stubborn destructive current practices within Islam that must be removed or modified. However, there appears to be great compatibility with the globalism narrative should certain beliefs and practices be abrogated (replaced). According to the Gospel of Globalism blending with Islam, Mohammed is a prototype of someone coming (The Mahdi) who could unite the people in such a way to remove the problem of religion and prepare humanity for its next phase of evolution- possibly a supernatural evolution. If only there was more Islamic scholarship on this subject.

Dealing with Judaism and Christianity

Even while waiting on this tantalizing possibility, Globalists view Islam (as is currently practiced today) as potentially really helpful in warring against the other dogmatic mono-theistic religions and preparing the earth for the right time when the Gospel of Globalism narrative can be openly displayed when the invisible "supernatural" realm has been harnessed under human control and is now predictable. The other religions- Judaism and Christianity present potentially a much larger challenge to the Gospel of Globalism narrative.

Judaism comes in several "flavors" reformed (or progressive) Judaism, conservative, and orthodox. Orthodox Judaism is the most problematic as they believe that their Messiah is literally coming to earth to rule and reign from David's throne while also literally believing the Torah is the very word of God- not to be tampered with. It is at the core of Jewish identity as a people group for thousands of years. (How they have survived for thousands of years as a distinct people group without a homeland is beyond sociological explanation. Why have they remained a distinct people group when it is much easier to assimilate?) This has led to a refusal to change their belief systems and it is their stubbornness that is a real problem to peace in the Middle East according to the globalism narrative.

From an overall globalism perspective, the number Orthodox Jews are thankfully quite small (versus the world population). Meanwhile, reformed Judaism is much more open to the progressive improvements that the globalism narrative offers. It must be added that many ethnically Jewish people are very secular or agnostic-who would clearly be open to the Gospel of globalism narrative.

The Gospel of Globalism narrative deals with the same problems with Christians as with Jewish people. The only difference between orthodox Jewish believers and Christian believers is that Christians believe their Messiah Jesus Christ, has already come. What is troubling is that many believe their messiah is the Jewish Messiah that will come again, but for various historical reasons, the Jewish people have rejected their own messiah! The problem is compounded in that there are many millions of Christians across the earth like this who believe this-and that there are large numbers of them-some in very influential positions in every part of society.

While there are millions of dogmatic Christians, Globalists are encouraged that many main-line denominations of Christianity are becoming much more "progressive" and open to change. These denominations are re-interpreting scripture in light of current events and trends. A great globalist victory came in 2009 when the

Evangelical Lutheran Church in America changed their stance of homosexuality, reinterpreting some of the ancient prohibitions. This was a bold step- even though surrounding events on the same day and time while the delegates voted was quite foreboding[4]. Martin Luther was the author of the protestant reformation that gave new understanding to Christianity. Perhaps much of Christianity is open to a second reformation more in line with globalist thinking.

Globalists laud the efforts of the current pope: Pope Francis of the Catholic Church. Here are a few quotes from St. Francis on the subject of globalism and the need for a unified global religion:

Today, this selfish attitude of indifference has taken on global proportions, to the extent that we can speak of a globalization of indifference. It is a problem which we, as Christians, need to confront.[5]

In promoting tolerance across every religion, Pope Francis celebrated the erecting of an ancient statue of the ancient god Molech outside the Roman Coliseum.

According to the Gospel of Globalism, Pope Francis is doing much to unite the world's religions in bringing goodwill and cooperation. He has also made some subtle changes to the Lord's prayer believing that current spirituality includes a higher power that is benevolent to all and does not lead people into temptation [6]. As an adherent to progressive Christianity, the Pope working to reconcile Christian theology with Islam:

Our relationship with the followers of Islam has taken on great importance, since they are now significantly present in many traditionally Christian countries, where they can freely worship and become fully a part of society. We must never forget that they

---

[4] https://en.wikipedia.org/wiki/2009_ELCA_Churchwide_Assembly accessed 7/29/2019
[5] *Pope Francis (2017). "Happiness in This Life: A Passionate Meditation on Material Existence and the Meaning of Life", p.86, Pan Macmillan* https://www.azquotes.com/quote/873800 *accessed 7/25/2019.*
[6] https://www.premier.org.uk/News/World/Pope-Change-the-Lord-s-Prayer accessed 7/25/2019

"profess to hold the faith of Abraham, and together with us they adore the one, merciful God, who will judge humanity on the last day"[7].

In summary, progressive Christianity, and progressive Judaism are actually in agreement with the Gospel of Globalism. A real hindrance to globalist dreams are the millions of Christians and Jews who believe God does not change and refuse to change their belief systems. They are going to force an empirical showdown.

Towards a spiritual showdown: the search for evidence.

The evidence of the unseen or "supernatural" affected the world today is growing but how? The globalist view is that the problem is a lack of knowledge (and ways to get that knowledge). Thus the operation of the unseen or "supernatural" appears to be quite random. However, powerful new technology may soon unlock this knowledge.

First, there is the CERN particle accelerator that seeks to smash atoms together at speeds approaching the speed of light safely and perhaps yield surprising results. We already discovered sub-atomic particles and that light behaves like a sub-atomic particle in one sense, but like waves in another sense. There have been discoveries of things such as "anti-matter" and dark matter. In addition, there is an increasing number of anecdotal stories that may give us some clues. Would secular globalists support more research among those who practice esoteric rituals with spirits?

While awaiting more empirical evidence, the reason why people flock to religion is that it gives clear definitions of "love" and "hate". Globalists continue to redefine love and hate- especially in regards to "hate speech": Saying and doing things that makes

---

[7] *Pope Francis (2014). "The Joy of the Gospel", p.69, BookBaby* *https://www.azquotes.com/author/5099-Pope_Francis/tag/islam accessed 7/25/2019.*

people "feel good" is love. Practicing tolerance is a generally a good thing from a globalist point of view.

Meanwhile, saying and doing things that offend other people needs to be condemned as "hate speech" and cannot be tolerated in a globalist society. Unfortunately, stubborn religious belief is the source of much "hate speech" in society. For example, the "hate speech" against the GLBT community is not to be tolerated in a globalist-run society. To globalists, avoiding intolerant hate speech is much more important than maintaining the freedom of religion.

A great spiritual hope of those who adhere to the globalism narrative is a greater understanding of what we now call "the supernatural" to harness and control it. Only 100 years ago, the idea of people flying into space, organ transplants, or landing on the moon appeared to be "supernatural". Perhaps the unseen "supernatural" and the natural realm DO operate together with some level of predictability. Is it possible to conquer and control these invisible "forces"? Victory would bring the great words of the poem Invictus to reality:

I am the master of my fate:
I am the captain of my soul[8]

Someday, humanity will be able to harness and control unseen powers (the 'supernatural powers') and use them to benefit humanity? With a greater understanding on how to use the unseen powers, it will be possible to confront those who have stubborn religious convictions that have caused a lot of problems for a New World Order. With clear empirical evidence, they then must evolve their belief systems or else, natural selection and evolution must be applied within humanity.

---

[8] Henley, William Earnest, *Invictus.* These words also represent Timothy McVeigh's (the 1994 Oklahoma City Bomber) last words.

Chapter 9:   The Gospel of Globalism- The end of all things

In the last chapter, we looked at who we are as humanity-specifically religion and spirituality. The humanist Gospel of Globalism narrative presents a vastly different view of spirituality, humanity, the problem of evil, and suffering to the Bible. The globalism narrative describes the problem of applied knowledge, the lack of collective knowledge of the invisible, "supernatural" realm, along with organized fundamentalist religion as the key sources of the problem-especially if confronted with empirical evidence (that currently globalists are in process of collecting). However, how is the Gospel of Globalism narrative supposed to end? Where is this going both individually and collectively?

The problem of death: What happens after it?

The Bible presents human sin and selfishness as the source of evil, pain, suffering, and death. God currently allows the presence of sin, evil, pain, suffering, and death in this age but it will not always be this way. This insurmountable problem is why Jesus came to the earth the first time- to make punitive atonement for human sin and make reconciliation to God and transformation into the likeness of Jesus possible. He defeated death but death has not been destroyed.

So where is this going collectively and individually? There is a day of reckoning coming when God will bring an end to sin, evil, suffering, and pain- but this means big trouble for everyone unless individual humans are counted righteous by God who is perfect in every way. The Bible promises that God will one day destroy the last enemy of humanity: death.

The Bible makes it clear what happens after death: God will one day raise the dead and all will be judged. The Bible warns that everyone will face judgment from God after death. (Revelation 20:11-15; Daniel 7: 9-17, 12:2-3; 2 Corinthians 5:9-10 etc.) The Bible also warns of eternal torment for those who choose their own way and reject God's provision of atonement and reconciliation through Jesus Christ: God will indeed give them the fulness of everything selfish humanity "wants" along with the ultimate end-result of sin and selfishness for all eternity. Yet the Bible promises eternal life and eternal rewards for those who faithfully love and follow Jesus- they get to live in fellowship with God!

Meanwhile, the globalist narrative continues to be uncertain about what happens after death: Many who have had "near death experiences" describe a tunnel of light, love, and peace. Some describe seeing their body lying dead and being aware of what was happening in the room at that moment. Still others describe a more sinister experience of darkness and fear. A few describe the experience of outright conscious torment. Is there life and conscience after death when the physical body is laid in the ground? There is an assumption that the inherent nature of humanity is good and all of humanity will end up going to "the good place". This is even symbolically presented by the reality TV show *Survivor* where after contestants are eliminated from the game, and their torch extinguished (symbolizing death); they go to a place of rest and comfort called "Ponderosa" (symbolizing a hoped-for afterlife).

The hope of humanism: Could technology one day help humanity avoid the Grim Reaper?

The Bible also promises that Jesus Christ is coming back to rule on the physical earth- and goes into great detail in describing the events around his return. Christians believe Jesus is also the fulfillment of Israel's prophetic promises for the Messiah and fulfilled much biblical prophecy at his first coming. Many of these biblical prophecies were humanly impossible to control by Jesus as a human when he walked on the earth. Since Jesus literally fulfilled so much Biblical prophecy at his first coming to earth, why would we not expect Jesus to fulfill the rest of Biblical prophecy at his 2nd coming?

Meanwhile, the Gospel of Globalism narrative surprisingly has an eschatology (end of the story) as well- some of it is general, but some of it is specific. First in dealing with the problem of evil and human suffering, the Gospel of Globalism narrative states that it is the lack of expanding our knowledge base and applying it. Even as I write this, the technology to overcome the typical human limitations of accessing knowledge and then applying it with skill are being designed.

Currently, we use computer-chipped cards to make financial transactions in many nations of the world. There are currently experiments related to inserting small computer chips under people's skin- if successful, this would allow societies to quickly go cashless. This would eliminate a lot of crime related to cash and currency-and make a better society theoretically. However, according to globalists, there are many more potential applications to chip implants that ought to be very exciting- chip implants may the next digital revolution coming- that may spark the next great leap in human evolutionary development.

Globalists look to the exponential increase in knowledge, and the development of artificial intelligence (AI) as a compass to our future. Already, it has been proven through the game of chess that artificial intelligence that is self-learning is able to thrash "brute force" chess programs (that look at billions of positions per second), let alone human competitors. In 1997, a chess computer program beat (for the first time), then world-champion Garry Kasparov. Since then, computer speeds have risen exponentially along with the development of AI. An AI computer program would crush a human player in chess as even the best chess players make the best moves (according to computer programs) only roughly 70-90% of the time on a good day. Could chess be a symbol of making life-decisions and computers programs along with AI help humans make "the best moves" in life for us?

The advanced AI technology is being developed today and will be implemented tomorrow. Imagine a day when computer implanted chips help stimulate the brain and help human beings to make "all the right moves"[i]. We are only now beginning to discover how the human mind works-and how computer aided technology can help it work immeasurably better. There are already reports of how computer-aided technology is helping those who could not walk due to paralysis suddenly walk due to assisting with the neuron transmitters from the brain.

Could humanity live forever? It would only be a matter of time as knowledge continued to explode exponentially to where AI and increasing nano technology could bond with human biology to prevent biological death within humanity (though this could also cause unforeseen problems[ii]). Gene therapy, artificial intelligence, and the increasing knowledge would first likely improve the quality of life by allowing those who were blind to be able to see and those who were lame to be able to walk like typical human beings.

This technology would give humans who have it such a big advantage over those who don't that it would virtually represent a next step in the evolution of the human species-even in its early stages. The potential to rapidly process information (at computer-like lightning speeds) and then make decisions (through enhanced computer implants allowing for processing all applicable information at lightning speeds) would give humanity a huge advantage in our many pursuits including the search for life on other planets, solving problems such as the threat of global warming or other environmental concerns, and the search for understanding spirituality.

However, this technology would be extremely dangerous and need to be carefully regulated by upright people who agree with the humanist, globalist worldview. It would be horrifying if this technology fell into the hands of those who are stubborn and religious. Perhaps an openly public mark of loyalty[iii] to this globalist humanist worldview and to those who control this technology would be merited as they would need to be proven trustworthy to our highest human ideals to be bestowed this type of enhanced, evolutionary power. How to get there? There is a two-part globalism plan: eliminate stubborn religious belief and a social credit system to prove loyal worthiness to take the next step and evolve.

The globalist plan to eliminate the problem of stubborn religious belief

In addition, to lack of ability to acquire and apply knowledge, the globalist narrative declares that the other part of the problem being stubborn religious belief and absolute truth claims with very weak empirical evidence-especially in monotheistic religions. Last chapter, we looked at the problem of Islam, Bible-based Christianity, and Orthodox Judaism-according to the globalist narrative. We also explained a bit how Islam is ironically, quite compatible with the Gospel of Globalism narrative. However, the way Islam is practiced today presents quite an obstacle to human progress-but work rapidly is occurring. It may take a horrendous war where the Islamic hope (as it is currently practiced) is completely obliterated, but some of the teachings of Islam related to abrogation are actually very helpful to understand the Gospel of Globalism narrative.

Biblical-based Christianity presents the largest challenge with the supernatural-and there is the problem that many Christians (especially in American culture) believe that bearing arms is a good thing. However, there is apparently a critical flaw: As mentioned in chapter 6 in forming today's global culture, a large number of young people became Christians in the 1970's, expecting "the end of the world" in their generation-but nothing has happened. Now the report from some of their top mission leaders is that the Christian message has touched almost every nation (ethnic group) as a witness as of 2019.

Those who adhere to the globalist narrative will soon apparently be able to resolve the "Christian problem" due to the empirical claim of Christianity found in Matthew 24. Jesus said in Matthew 24:14;

"And this gospel of the kingdom will be preached in all the world as a witness to all the nations, and then the end will come." (Matthew 24:14)

When the announcement is made by their leaders (or leaked...in which case the globalists will say it) that the Christian message has gone to every ethnic group, most Christians will be expecting something apocalyptic to occur on a global scale (perhaps related to all of those films where millions of people are suddenly missing?) - well beyond renewed religious enthusiasm. After a few years go by and nothing apocalyptic happens, those who adhere to the globalist narrative will hopefully have much greater understanding of hidden "supernatural" or "spiritual" things. When better theories become available, the globalists will then apparently be able to gloat that Christianity has been proven as empirically false[iv] because "the end" did not come- and sway these hundreds of millions of disillusioned Christians to believe in the humanist globalist narrative through enhanced understanding of spirituality combined with the technological breakthroughs.

The other problem is dealing with the firearms of the Christians in America. However, the tide may be turning against "the right to bear arms" in America with so many reports of mass-shootings caused by bitter people who have guns. Through shrewd legislative maneuvering and strategic public campaigning, globalists think that they can convince the population majority of the United States that overturning the right to bear arms is a good thing.

In dealing with Orthodox Judaism, it will be more difficult for globalists to confront, but there is a way: Orthodox Jews are expecting their Messiah- the temple must be built in Jerusalem to their technical specifications; but this would infuriate hundreds of millions of devout Muslims- who are not hesitant to wage jihad (holy war) given the right circumstances.

According to the globalist narrative, there must be a way to disarm Islamic Jihadism and break their will to fight. However, this will likely involve a massive global crisis and war. Globalists do not want this to happen IMMEDIATELY after an announcement (or leak) that the Christian gospel is now in every ethnic group- or the problem of biblical Christianity will not be extinguished. A wait of a few years after executing this part of the strategy of falsifying obstinate Christianity would be advisable to maximize the case for globalism before seriously attempting to disarm Islamic Jihadism and breaking their will to fight[v] humanistic globalism. After breaking their will to fight, those who adhere to the Gospel of Globalism would be able to show how this narrative is compatible with the highest hopes of Islam- that Mohammed hinted at in the Quran.

Back to dealing with Orthodox Judaism and the temple: After a huge crisis that addresses the problem of Islamic Jihadism as it is currently understood, globalist humanists believe that the rebuilt temple could be a powerful symbol of how moral relativism, tolerance, and the acquisition of knowledge have triumphed to produce where everything and everyone else has failed: the achievement of peace and safety in the Middle East[vi]. The problem is finding just the right leader to broker this ultimate peace deal-who could at least somewhat fit the description of Judaism's promised Messiah. He must have family origins associations in Bethlehem, Nazareth, and Egypt. He must be incredibly brilliant intellectually and possess incredible human charisma, while also possessing understanding (and maybe even some control) of the "spiritual" or "supernatural" as well.

In addition, for globalistic humanists, building the third temple in Jerusalem would also be a grand (rigged) spiritual "science experiment" for all the world to see. The simple empirical way to prove orthodox Judaism (and their supposed covenant) is false is to build their temple to the specifications written in their prophets -but simply adjust the some of the key dimensions ever so slightly[vii]. Should nothing happen- then the world can easily see their God is not real. After this globalist humanists will then possess apparent empirical proof that Orthodox Judaism is false.

What if something "supernatural" happens? By manipulating the temple dimensions ever so slightly, there would then be proof that their God lied contradicting a fundamental tenant of Jewish Torah that God cannot lie (Numbers 23:19). There are statements in the Torah and other Hebrew prophets about the absolute requirements of the dimensions of the coming temple [viii]. In this case, there would be empirical proof that Orthodox Judaism is false.

Of course, there are some who will not change their minds- even in the face of convincing openly displayed evidence-who stubbornly refuse to evolve their belief systems to conform to the Globalism narrative. With these obstinate ones, it would perhaps be necessary to "help" natural selection and the evolutionary "survival of the fittest" dimensions to take care of them[ix]- and use them as a public display of the superiority of the globalism narrative over stubborn religious fundamentalism and to warn others not to go down this path. After all, this action is morally consistent with evolutionary moral relativism.

The dream of achieving the highest globalism hopes.

As stated last chapter, there is "something out there" that needs to be dealt with. Globalists believe that advanced technology such as the CERN particle accelerator and experiments conducted in other places on the earth (Area 51?) will unlock the nature of matter- what is part of the unseen "supernatural" today can be harnessed for the good of humanity. Consider how radio waves or the idea of transplanting human organs was viewed only 120 years ago. According to the globalism narrative, what do people think is really possible in the next 120 years?

Globalists would say, "Imagine harnessing the synergy of AI technology, implanted computer technology, and understanding the hidden "supernatural" realm harnessed in ways that keep our physical bodies alive indefinitely and keep our bodies physically healthy and functioning. Imagine this technology allowing us to process knowledge and apply it perfectly at an exponentially accelerated way in growing food, engineering our physical environment, and the pursuit of building other technological innovations and inventions." Humanity could then virtually build a utopia on the earth using the best of technology, the best "hidden knowledge", and best human wisdom and intuition.

In addition, evolved human technology along with the increased use of Virtual reality (VR) could allow for evolved human beings to experience every dream and pleasure they have longed for in VR. Imagine VR experiences that are so real-that you can barely tell the difference between reality and VR. This would allow people to experience things such as winning a championship in sports, eating the best food, or any other ultimate fantasy. Imagine also what happens if whole communities of people could link up and experience these VR pleasures together?

Building a physical utopia is the easy part- a much more difficult task would be building a relational utopia related to how we interact with each other. Those who adhere to the gospel of globalism would argue that all of this coming new technology and knowledge could then apply this technology to build an offense-free society...yet at the same time expressing the beauty of human diversity. Imagine relatively perfectly applied knowledge in a society city where everyone knows how to avoid offending everyone and anyone due to knowing what offends individuals? Who would need religion, family, or marriage[x]- to adherents of the gospel of globalism, these are simply boundaries to road blocks to the fullest expression of "adult experiences". This would cause an unprecedented level of unity in this "evolved" human race.

In order for this to happen, a prototype city would need to be built, far more advanced than Dubai. It might sound elitist to say this, but only those who have been entrusted and implanted with this evolutionary technology would be eligible to live in this ultra-luxurious prototype city of evolved human beings. Imagine this beautiful luxurious city in the heart of the Middle East like Iraq as a symbol of victory over dogmatic religious belief[xi]. Imagine evolved human citizens with evolved special technology, who are connected by brain implants (allowing lightning fast collection and applied use of knowledge), harnessing the hidden powers of the unknown, and all with a common vision of building an offense-free society where everyone experiences the best pleasures this world can offer. Would everyone have an opportunity to earn their way in? Theoretically, the answer is yes.

The globalist dream of an evolved, unified human race with diversity could then tackle questions such as spontaneously creating life by getting all the biological interactions right. Globalists dream of the exponential growth of total knowledge, the technologically aided ability to humanly process and apply large amounts of knowledge into the situation. With high-level evolved technology, Journeying to new star systems and colonizing them with human life and even exploring whether other atomic processes could produce life would now be part of the realm of imagination and possibility.

With the globalist dreams fulfilled, why would people need a deity? The exponential growth of applied knowledge would triumph over the need to follow a deity. With the ultimate fulfillment of these globalist dreams, perhaps this would be proof that man could basically function as their own god[xii]. Death would no longer be feared as people could (theoretically) live forever due to coming technology. People with the ability to control their reality and environment could be proof to the globalists that people ate from the right tree-supposedly at the beginning.

The Globalist social strategy on moving toward utopian society

How would the natural selection process go about to see who would be eligible for this breakthrough technology and merit bestowing such a gift? Globalists are carefully watching the social experiment of Communist China and the construction of a "Social Credit Score" system. Basically, the Chinese government (through the funding of big technology firms) has purchased millions of video cameras that watch everything its citizens do. In addition, it is possible to record events and information through the use of cell phones, credit cards, and other technology to track where everyone in China is and what everyone in mainland China does.

The government authorities then reward behavior that it then approves of by assigning a higher "social credit scores". Examples of virtuous behavior would include volunteering for the Communist Party, practice courtesy, work productively, and exposing organized behavior the government disapproves of (such as hidden cults) etc. or serving the will of people with higher social credit scores. However, the government then penalizes behavior (that is not overtly criminal) by lowering a person's social credit score for doing things such as littering, loitering and misusing time, and attending unauthorized gatherings (such as suspected house churches). The final credit score then has huge implications on where people stand within Chinese society.

Those with low credit scores would be unable to travel or send their children to good schools. Those with low credit scores would only be able to take certain jobs that are lower status in the eyes of the collective Chinese society-regardless of academic and technical qualifications. Meanwhile, those with higher social credit scores have a wider access to jobs with higher status roles and greater financial pay. Those with higher credit schools are granted ability to travel abroad and receive other perks of the Chinese society. The highest social credit scores enable those who hold them, to access to top luxury hotels, special events, and other amenities-

along with the ability to send their children to the most prestigious schools.

Perfected, this technology has several advantages: history has shown that economics are a far more powerful motivator than simply making laws for most people. Americans typically vote their pocketbooks- what leaders and philosophy will help me gain what I want? Second, this will make for a much safer society-any criminal acts will likely be caught on camera (or tri-angulated by digital technology) and the perpetrators will experience justice; including a lowered credit score, but so much more can then be done. Third, this will free government resources and people to deal with what is clearly greater threats to the dream society such as eliminating the problem of dogmatic religion.

Finally, a system of social credit scoring could also be used to determine who has earned the right to take a public mark of loyalty on their right hand or forehead to take part in this evolutionary computer technology-and earn their way into the evolutionary, prototype city. It would take a history of ambition and loyalty to win the right to take this mark-but this innovation would theoretically be open to all of humanity.

This is a summary of the Gospel of Globalism as a prescription to deal with the ills of humanity. If you are inspired to this new Gospel of Globalism narrative, turn the pages to find out how the Globalist elites attempting to build a new world order will react to your new-found globalist beliefs.

If you choose to believe this, the reaction of the "friendly globalist elites" will ultimately be similar to how the Communist socialists were planning to react to their new converts:

"[T]he useful idiots, the leftists who are idealistically believing in the beauty of the Soviet socialist or Communist or whatever system, when they get disillusioned, they become the worst enemies. That's why my KGB instructors specifically made the point: never bother with leftists. Forget about these political prostitutes. Aim higher. [...] They serve a purpose only at the stage of destabilization of a nation. For example, your leftists in the United States: all these professors and all these beautiful civil rights defenders. They are instrumental in the process of the subversion only to destabilize a nation. When their job is completed, they are not needed any more. They know too much. Some of them, when they get disillusioned, when they see that Marxist-Leninists come to power—obviously they get offended—they think that they will come to power. That will never happen, of course. They will be lined up against the wall and shot."
— **Yuri Bezmenov:** (A journalist who defected from the former USSR)

In other words, a sarcastic "Congratulations" is in order.

Did you notice footnotes? The gospel of globalism narrative was already foreseen and written about roughly 1900-2500 years ago and the United States is not a lead nation recorded in the book. Here is a partial list of where some of these noted items in the last chapter are predicted or talked about in the Bible.

Revelation 13:16-18/Revelation 14:9-11
ii Revelation 9:3-7
iii Revelation 13:16-18.
iv 2 Peter 3:1-6; A careful examination of Matthew 28:18-20; Revelation 5:9-10 is required.
v Daniel 8:1-8; 9:27
vi 1 Thessalonians 5:1-3
vii Revelation 11:1.
viii Contradicting Numbers 23:19
viii See Ezekiel 40-47; especially 41:1-4; 43:13-17; is this the secret defiling of the temple of Daniel 8:13-14?
ix Revelation 13:15
x 1 Timothy 4:3; Psalm 2:1-3
xi Revelation 17:1-8; Zechariah 5:5-11
xii Genesis 3:1-5

By embracing the Gospel of Globalism you need to ask yourself, "why am I eating from the tree of the knowledge of good and evil"?

Chapter 10: Implications for 2020 (and beyond)

As we approach the 2020 presidential election, this "gospel of globalism" narrative is a major underlying factor in American Politics. We can observe in crude ways, how the gospel of globalism narrative can use recent economic, technological, and societal progress to make the case that this is the right way to understand reality.

Implications for the 2020 election

The Gospel of Globalism narrative will likely deeply affect the 2020 Presidential election. President Trump won in 2016 against globalist-backed Hilary Clinton causing outrage among the entertainment, economic, and cultural elite. He has put America first in economic and military deals, angering many of long-standing NATO (North Atlantic Trade Organization) members from the Cold-War Era. Meanwhile, he has said things domestically that are clearly "politically incorrect". People have accused Trump (and those he appointed as part of his leadership team) of being sexist, racist, and homophobic. President Trump is looked at as the ultimate hero for some in America-as returning the United States back to its foundations in order to "keep America great".

Meanwhile, globalism advocates look at Donald Trump as the ultimate villain and stumbling block to their desires. In a 2018 interview with the Washington Post, George Soros rather angrily indicated that Donald Trump is destroying the New World Order. Most globalists adhere to the gospel of globalism narrative I have been describing in the last few chapters. There is a presumption that the United States of America will lead this globalism push- and maintain its role as the #1 nation in the world. For them, the Gospel of Globalism narrative to be the guide to world peace and prosperity. To the globalists, President Trump is a huge problem as he stands for the United States with nationalist positions, and not for progressive, globalist interests.

Why haven't the globalists attempted to assassinate Donald Trump? There are a few main reasons: First, how to do that? Assassination attempts generally do not get publicized due to people wanting to make a name for themselves (even if it is in infamy). All but any truly high-level, sophisticated attempts are generally sniffed out by the Secret Service before there is actually a threat. Second, assassination would not tip the balance of executive power in America due to what is written in the United States Constitution unless it was possible to take out the President and Vice President at the same time.

Third and perhaps most importantly, any successful high-level assassination by the globalists would only cause Donald Trump to be viewed as a martyr by many and the globalists to be viewed as a truly dangerous enemy. This would rally millions of nationalists and many who are "independent thinkers" to defend the United States from the globalist cause. A civil war between nationalists and globalists on the soil of the United States would ruin the U.S. globalist hope that the United States leads the New World Order and leave a global power vacuum for other nations such as China to take advantage of.

While the Democratic candidate for President is not yet known, we can clearly look at how the gospel of globalism narrative will influence the 2020 election in a few ways. The political battle lines are already being drawn and some of the alliances are actually pretty surprising- that go against typical United States political thinking. (i.e the rich are generally Republican while the poor favor Democrats). Many of the key issues of our day are indeed complex with different conflicting values that influence our views on what we should do to tackle these difficult problems. However, there is a clear agenda behind some of these issues. We need to take a look at the Gospel of Globalism position and the underlying agenda on some key domestic issues that will shape the 2020 United States general election.

Domestic politics

a. *Health care-*

Health care is about the relief of human suffering, and well-being of people. Globalists will argue that a major overhaul is needed as the current health care systems favor some people over others- that many are being left out. Their solution will be to offer free health care for everyone (including abortion on demand)- likely in the form of a single-payer health care system. While the problems are complex and people really suffer due to lack of health insurance and affordable health care, relieving human suffering is not the primary issue from the globalist point-of view. The underlying goal of a globalist agenda is to get the general population dependent upon the globalist elites for one of the most personal issues people will ever face-their personal health and well-being.

"Control the health care and you control the people"- Saul Alinksy; *Rules for Radicals*

b. *Immigration*

The great wealth disparity between the United States and Mexico does create problems with border crossings. Those who hold to a Gospel of Globalism narrative will promote "open borders" and "global citizenship". This also includes giving free health care and other citizenry benefits to illegals in the name of "fairness for the poor". The underlying globalist motive is not a desire to honor other cultures or ease human suffering at the border. The underlying real issue is that nationalist governments are an obstacle that must be overcome to unifying the world under a global government. The open borders and "global citizenry" agenda promotes the globalism narrative, weaken the U.S. economy, and promote the re-distribution of wealth away from nations that oppose globalism.

c. *Gun Control*

Citing the spate of recent mass-shootings by "crazed" people with some sort of grudge, there is an increased call to restrict (and then possibly end) the right to bear arms guaranteed by the 2nd Amendment. The globalist position on the right to bear arms is that all guns should be registered and only those who are qualified as "mentally fit" (i.e. agreement with the globalist ideology and values) should have the right to bear arms.

d. *Taxes and the economy:*

The mantra of globalism will be some variation of "tax the rich to help take care of the poor". Globalists will argue that like Robin hood, we need to give hand-outs to the poor and the oppressed by taking from the rich. On the surface, this sounds like a heroic idea to ease suffering and administer social justice.

This mantra sounds good and just but it is very deceptive. The real goal is to make the majority of the population dependent upon government aid and the financial elites-and thus more controllable ideologically. This was the strategy of Socialist Communism. (Everyone knows that it is not good to bite the hand that feeds you.) Yet why would globalists want to tax the rich (i.e. presumably themselves) more?

The answer is simple: "The rich" that globalist adherents want to tax more heavily are the middle class, upper-middle class, and the millionaires- not *the multi-billionaires or trillionaires (individuals or corporations) that control the global economy or champion globalism*. The globalist financial elites that finance governments are able to "lawyer up" or lobby to change laws so they can strategically invest their finances in ways to make them immune to higher income tax brackets that they propose upon "the rich". The underlying goal is to both expand their global reach and eliminate potential competition to their financial power-bases (in the form of the millionaire individuals or companies that are worth hundreds of millions of dollars, but are not in agreement with the globalism agenda ideologically).

e. *"Moral issues" (legalization of recreational drugs, abortion, homosexuality)-*

The globalism position is: the more freedom- the better. Sexual expression should not be hindered by "religious rules from the Church" that have affected United States society. The continuation of legalized abortion is particularly important for the globalist agenda to control "unwanted populations", redefine justice as focusing on the quality of life, and re-define family structures. Many globalists believe all "illegal" drugs should be legal as long as they don't hurt anyone. Legalization and then controlling access to these recreational drugs could be another way to control the ideology of the population. (Meanwhile the biblical positions on these moral issues are very clear.)

To the globalists, the main reasons for taking these positions on key moral issues is to undermine biblical family structures and values, change the laws of the land to reflect secular rule of law, and remove the expression of Christianity in public (the biggest resistance to their complete take-over) within the United States. From history, they can see that the Russian Communists were unable to stay in power because in part, the family structure was kept intact. The cultural revolution destroyed the family structures in China and the Chinese Communists remain firmly in control, in spite of capitalist economic reforms.

International politics:

Those who adhere to the Gospel of Globalism will also several key positions in promoting global government in U.S. foreign policy. For example, globalists emphasize the danger of global warming and climate change-that something must be done by a global government because nations do things in the interest of their nation at the potential expense of wrecking life for the whole human race.

Much of Europe's high-level leadership (with the exception of Great Britain and the whole BREXIT mess) embraces a Gospel of Globalism narrative with the European Union (EU) at the center of the New World Order. Globalists in the United States will advocate close partnership with the EU including embracing their social and economic ideologies (humanism, socialism). Meanwhile, Europe is increasingly being influenced by Sunni Islam due to mass-immigration and rapid reproductive rate in the Islamic culture.

A real potential point of contention is regarding the homosexual agenda: Globalists embrace this as the "fullest expression of human sexuality"-even to the point of redefining what family to include them. Meanwhile Islam (along with biblical Christianity and Orthodox Judaism) sharply condemn homosexuality as sexual immorality. Again, a key for Islam related to this issue is the doctrine of abrogation where "new revelation" can ultimately supplant older revelation and their historic position on this.

Look for globalists to prepare the United States, Europe, and other nations for a massive war by labeling Russia, China, Iran (and maybe others) as "immoral", "oppressive", and "dangerous" (It is well known that Russia has military alliances with China and Iran). However, in the same token, the globalists will likely secretly help fund (or give technology for) Russia, China, Iran, and its global "proxy partners" to launch limited strikes against western targets in the coming years in order to slowly build up tension until the time is right to "release the tension" in the form of a world war. The underlying goal is to break Islam as we know it-and then assimilate parts of it into the gospel of globalism. Remember, due to a core doctrine of abrogation (replacement theology), Islam is potentially very compatible with the Gospel of Globalism narrative.

We looked at the underlying reason last chapter of a coming world war to realign the nations. Globalists will generally support the BDS movement against Israel as they view Israel's intolerant religious beliefs and religious ties to the land as a significant problem. The end-goal is bringing a covenant peace to the Middle East (specifically regarding Israel and Jerusalem) as the ultimate triumph of the Gospel of Globalism narrative over intolerant religions; something the Bible predicts.

Implications for the Church:

What should Christians actually do? Let's start with what to avoid: The Church must not look at Donald Trump's presidency (whether he is re-elected in 2020 or not) with "messianic" hopes for the United States. No human being, no matter how gifted, talented, wealthy, or brash is the ultimate answer for the United States. The Bible is clear that God sets government leaders in place for his own sovereign purposes and for the benefit of the people (Daniel 2:20; 2 Thessalonians 2:1-8 etc). Paul said that God set Nero in place as emperor over Rome (who was killing Christians)! In the end, it is God who will enable the "man of lawlessness", a globalist, to seize power for his own purposes- including completing the Biblical narrative.

In the last three chapters, we have looked at how the coming Gospel of Globalism will attempt to answer three key identity questions that all humanity must grapple with. I presented their arguments in a rather limited and crude way. The real Gospel of Globalism narrative presentation will be much more sophisticated, seductive, and with better sounding arguments. The Gospel of Globalism will come with demonstrations of evil power of augmented technology, endorsements from governmental, economic, and cultural leaders, and even "supernatural" signs and wonders that can be explained with the Gospel of Globalism narrative. Though there are many biblical ways to resist the Gospel of Globalism, I want to highlight four practical applications:

1.   *Seek to understand the Biblical narrative.*

On the surface, it is easy to see how this false secular narrative is easily refutable by an understanding of the Bible. The Gospel of Globalism presents a way for man to become their own god and then fulfill their wildest dreams through evolved technology and exponential knowledge growth. The Bible warns that this is basically the same lie that satan presented to Adam and Eve in the Garden of Eden. Ministries such as the Center for Biblical End-Time studies (CBETS) are forming to help the Church understand the end of the biblical narrative in much greater detail.

The problem with most under 40 in the United States, is they are biblically illiterate. In addition, among self-professing, progressive Christians, many do no not believe the Bible is the inerrant, inspired word of God (in the original texts) and is ultimately authoritative for people who follow Jesus. If we do not embrace the biblical narrative, the default of human nature (due to the incident in the Garden of Eden) is selfishness at the expense of others. This will cause us to embrace this false Gospel of Globalism narrative. The Gospel of Globalism narrative appeals to our human desire for greatness and apparently infinite pleasure. It appeals to our desire to learn and achieve without long-term suffering or pain.

2.   *We need to embrace the Author of the biblical narrative deeply.*

Biblical "head" knowledge alone is not enough to overcome the Gospel of Globalism. Intellectually understanding the global biblical narrative will not be enough to make the right decisions when the pressure is on. Jesus rebuked the religious leaders for not discerning the times and the seasons. Given the huge error the religious leaders made at Jesus' first coming, how can we be sure that we won't make the same mistake at Jesus' second coming related to the Gospel of Globalism narrative?

Paul noted that those who do not love the truth will end up deceived while those who love the truth will end up getting the whole truth. Truth is a person (John 14:6). The Bible declares we can directly know the Author of the biblical narrative who is named "Faithful and True". Jesus promised the Spirit of Truth to come and guide people into all truth. Deeply understanding the biblical narrative requires a deep intimate knowledge with the Author himself-something the Bible declares God deeply desires.

3. *Listen!*

Refuting the Gospel of Globalism narrative requires more than simply Bible knowledge and reasoning. Intimate relationship with the Author is also essential. However, these two things alone will not win the hearts of a broken generation. In presenting the Gospel of Globalism, I presented typical intellectual arguments (many with unsound logic) used to promote this false narrative. However, behind the intellectual arguments is a lot of pain and heartache- often in the form of judgmentalism and condemnation based on perception of truth, but not The Truth. Do we have ears to hear to understand how to bring open demonstrations of "The Truth" that will set people free?

4. *Be in communities that seek to partner with the Supernatural God*

It is impossible to address large problems posed by this false Gospel of Globalism individually. Rugged individualism will not work. What is needed are communities of people connected with God and one another. The glory of God's wisdom is that it does not depend on a centralized hierarchy like most political governments. God can suddenly raise up whoever he wants both within a small community and whatever community he wants within a fellowship of communities in a city or within the wider Body of Christ. Winning the heart of a generation will require the practical demonstration of the supremacy of the Biblical gospel narrative over the Gospel of Globalism narrative *by communities.*

While the gospel of globalism narrative sounds seductive and even intimidating to those who love Truth, God will NOT be out done by a false gospel of globalism. Satan, humanism, or anything else is merely creation- with no chance of defeating the Creator. The only arena anyone can compete with God in (because he allows it) is in the realm of wisdom. The Bible describes two types of wisdom: There is wisdom that is worldly, human, and leads to every wicked thing along with destruction. Then there is wisdom that comes from heaven. The key question: which type of wisdom will produce the superior pleasure to the human heart?

God is setting up a show-down before the heavens and the earth. There is a false Gospel of Globalism narrative and a biblical gospel narrative. God will let the fullness of humanistic, worldly wisdom come forth (and the resulting societal impacts) as a backdrop to display the beauty, majesty, and victory of God's wisdom through the Church. The mercy, righteousness, and justice of God will be made known through the global family that he raises up. In the end, the Bride of Christ will be made ready; the bride act like Jesus, and speak like Jesus, and even shine like Jesus. God's people will have the honor of vindicating the wisdom of God forever. To begin this process, we (whether within the United States or outside of it) must resist the Gospel of Globalism.

About the author: Jess Gjerstad

Born in 1976 in Pusan South Korea, Jess Gjerstad was rescued and adopted into the United States. Jess was raised in a Christian family and grew up in the Lutheran Church.

In 1990, Jess had a life-changing encounter with Jesus Christ. This was the first of many supernatural encounters. He also began to sense a call from God to full-time occupational ministry.

In 2003, God called Jess to leave Minnesota and everything familiar to live in Kansas City. Jess joined the staff at the International House of Prayer (IHOP-KC) in 2003 where he continues to the present. In 2004, Jess earned his Masters of Divinity from Bethel Seminary in St. Paul, Minnesota.

If you are interested for Jess to come and speak at your church or conference, email authorjessgjerstad@gmail.com

www.ingramcontent.com/pod-product-compliance
Lightning Source LLC
Chambersburg PA
CBHW031249250726
48655CB00005B/2142